BRENT LIBRARIES

Please return/renew this item
by the last date shown.
Books may also be renewed by
phone or online.
Tel: 0333 370 4700
On-line www.brent.gov.uk/libraryservice

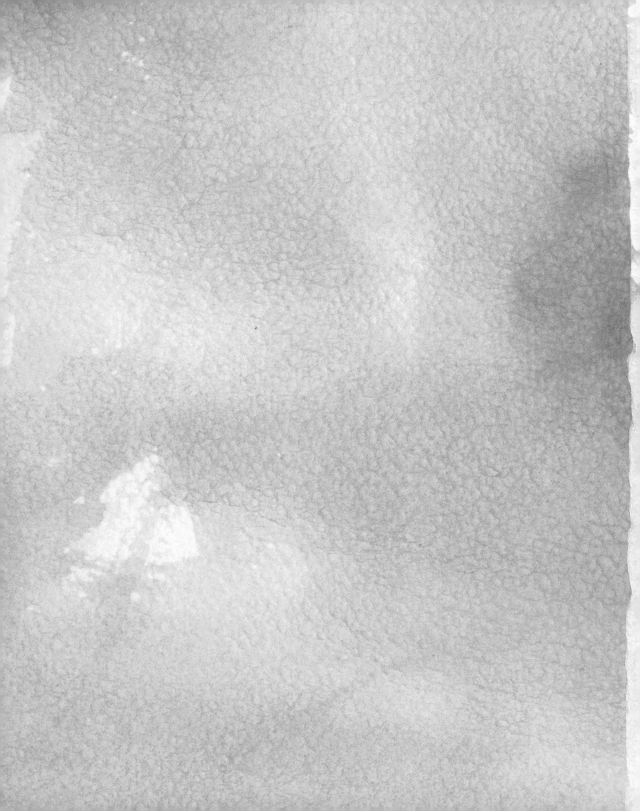

NATHAN OUTLAW'S FISH KITCHEN

Foreword by
HESTON BLUMENTHAL
Photography by DAVID LOFTUS

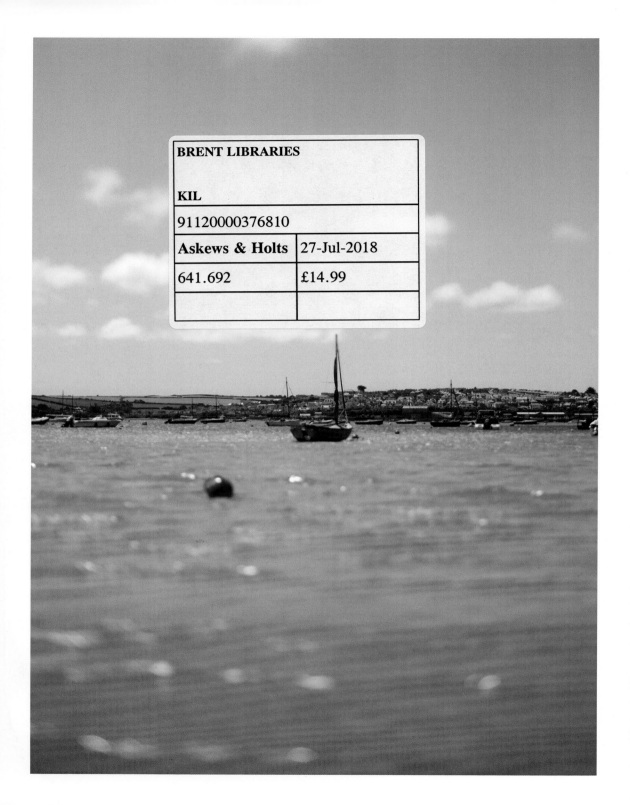

FOREWORD

I have a couple of early, very fond memories of Nathan. The first is from when I was judging a competition in which he was taking part. He served up a risotto that was so beautifully balanced, it stopped me in my tracks and I remember thinking, this chef's definitely going somewhere. Since then, he has opened several restaurants, including Restaurant Nathan Outlaw, which has become one of the best restaurants in the country, and Outlaw's Fish Kitchen in Port Isaac, which has to be one of the most charming restaurants I've eaten in. So I guess my assessment of his skill was pretty accurate.

The second is from a visit to the restaurant at the Lords of the Manor hotel in the Cotswolds when Nathan was working as a sous chef there under John Campbell. I arrived pushing my son, Jack, in a wheelchair because he'd managed to break a leg. Nathan had a couple of hours off that afternoon, and instantly decided to take Jack off for a bout of fishing in the grounds of the hotel.

These pictures give, I think, some insight into the kind of chef Nathan is – determined, generous and a great culinary technician. His devotion to all things fishy is second to none. He has thought carefully about how best to cook and present the produce of our rivers and seas, and worked hard at perfecting his craft. As a result, his dishes have – as you'll see – a real elegance to them: subtle and beautifully balanced, respectful of tradition and precisely executed. On the plate, his cooking has a real simplicity, but it's been forged from a total obsession with his craft and a fascination for how ingredients go together.

Nathan's dedication to seeking out the best and freshest local produce is impressive. He knows Cornwall inside out and has sought out loads of fantastic local suppliers and developed enduring relationships with them. This is one of the keys to Nathan's success: his cooking is driven and inspired by what's fresh, what's local and what's available, and you can really taste Cornwall in his food.

Nathan's warmth and his compassion shine through his cooking and through this book. His enthusiasm and down-to-earth attitude make him an excellent guide to cooking fish and seafood. The recipes have a restraint that will appeal to the inexperienced cook but, equally, they have plenty of complexity of flavour and variety of texture to satisfy the more adventurous. I'm especially pleased to see page space given to techniques like pickling, smoking and curing, which are all great favourites of mine but have, until recently, been largely ignored. *Nathan Outlaw's Fish Kitchen* contains lots of vibrant, sophisticated dishes to excite and inspire – take a look and I think you'll be hooked!

HESTON BLUMENTHAL

CONTENTS

INTRODUCTION

People often ask me how I keep coming up with new dishes. The answer isn't straightforward, but to keep at the top of my game and to satisfy my creativity my cooking has to continuously evolve. Some of my favourite times in my kitchens are when I get together with the guys to discuss and try out ideas for new dishes. Sometimes a supplier brings in something that triggers my imagination. I think to myself, 'That would be nice with...', or I draw on my classical training or experiences I've had eating elsewhere; then again a new dish may emerge from a happy accident!

Whatever the source of the idea, the recipes in this book are for dishes I've created and love to cook both in the restaurant kitchens and at home. And the key is that they are simple to prepare, based on sustainable species and all made with ingredients you can shop for easily.

I want you to use this book, not just put it on a shelf! I want you to realise that cooking fish and seafood is not as difficult as many people seem to think. To make life easier I've divided the recipes into chapters according to the way each dish is cooked – or just prepped in the case of raw dishes.

For each chapter, I have given you information about the technique used that will help you to understand what happens to the seafood as you follow the recipe, thus enabling you to get fantastic results. I've also indicated the varieties of fish and shellfish that respond best to each technique and suggested appropriate accompaniments and garnishes, so that you wow those you are cooking for every time.

To give you an insight into my style of cooking, I've covered all the techniques I use. I like to think I'm not a stereotypical chef. I don't have signature dishes, I do not make demands on my fishermen or suppliers, and I don't cook food that is complicated. My dishes may be complex in terms of their flavour and texture combinations, but they are really not overly complicated to prepare. That's the secret!

So, how do I decide what I'm going to cook? Local seafood is, of course, my main source of inspiration. For me, creating a dish always starts with the fish or shellfish. That definitely has to be 'the star of the show'. Then I look to the other produce that is available to me and in season, using only the best quality – that way I can be sure of great results. Unlike meat and poultry, seafood is highly seasonal, so it is variable and it isn't always available when you'd like it to be. I've learnt to deal with this by taking a flexible approach to my cooking, mixing and matching where necessary.

Some of my most successful dishes have been born out of adversity – for instance, when a particular fish hasn't been landed due to bad weather. (The smaller boats can't get out when the weather is bad.) I am always thinking about food, forever learning about food and, most critically, always tasting it as I cook.

Every type of seafood is different. Even the same species will respond differently depending on the way you cook it – or don't as the case may be. It varies according to size, where it is from and how it's been caught. Using the seasons to full advantage is the best starting point, but I also want to give you a few tips and tricks that will enable you to take seafood to another level, without losing its beautiful purity and character. Acidity and salt are seafood's best friends – their balance is vital to the success of a dish; confidence, practice and tasting are the only ways to get these right.

I can understand the fear of cooking fish and seafood: it has bones; it smells; it has a slimy appearance and sometimes it's alive! I've therefore made it my mission to remove the fear, mystery and awkwardness that surround seafood cookery. With practice, prepping fish yourself and dealing with the bones isn't difficult – just follow my step-by-step guides to the different varieties (see pages 182–211), or befriend a good fishmonger who will happily do it for you. Next, follow my recipes and you'll see that it really isn't something to be fearful of.

As for it being smelly, really fresh fish should have an inviting aroma of the sea; it will only have an unpleasantly 'fishy' smell if it's not in good condition. And you can avoid lingering fishy odours after cooking if you wrap up the skin, bones and leftovers immediately and put them straight in an outside bin - not in your kitchen food bin. A great tip for you: after prepping fish, rinse your hands and preparation equipment – board, knives, etc. – in cold water first, then hot. If you use warm or hot water first it will cook the fish residue, which then sticks to your skin, boards etc., making them smell.

Contrary to what you might think, slime is a good sign. If it's absent, it suggests the fishmonger or shopkeeper may have washed it off to make the fish more presentable, possibly because it's not as fresh as it should be. The slime is easily washed off, but again, use cold water.

Don't be put off by seafood that's alive. Think about it: it's the freshest way you can get it. As long as you do that seafood justice, it should be an honour and pleasure to cook and eat it, not something to be afraid of. If you don't like to see it wriggling or moving about, then all I can say is 'man up and get over it'. This is great seafood!

It's well known that fish and seafood are a healthy food choice. It is recommended that we eat at least two portions per week, one of which should be oily fish. Personally, I think that's not enough, but then I would say that! Joking aside, all seafood is a very good source of protein and many vitamins and minerals.

Oily fish are particularly beneficial as they have the added bonus of omega-3 fatty acids, which can help keep your heart, joints, skin and eyes healthy, and (as my nan used to tell me when I was a child) boost your brainpower! Obviously, coating the fish in batter and deep-frying it isn't great, but there are plenty of healthier cooking methods to choose from which can be just as, if not more, delicious. Oily fish, such as whitebait, anchovies and tinned sardines, can be eaten whole, bones and all, which is good for our bones as they're an excellent source of calcium and phosphorus.

White fish is very low in fat, making it a much better source of protein than most red and processed meats, which tend to be high in fat, particularly unhealthy saturated fat. Similarly, shellfish is also low in fat and a good source of zinc, iodine, copper and selenium. Mussels, oysters and crab, in particular, contain omega-3 fatty acids, though not as much as oily fish.

However, you should be aware that you can overdo it with oily fish, so it's advisable to eat no more than four or five portions a week. If you are pregnant that needs to reduce to a couple of portions. Unfortunately, this is down to pollutants found in oily fish. A little word of warning about swordfish (not featured in this book), which should be avoided totally by pregnant woman because it contains higher levels of mercury than other fish. If you're not pregnant then the recommendation is that it is alright to eat one or two portions of swordfish per week.

As far as white fish is concerned, it is ok to eat as much as you like; however, if eating bream, bass and turbot be aware that these can contain low levels of pollutants too, so it's not wise to eat them every day. With shellfish, you can pretty much go for it, but take it easy with brown crab meat.

Sustainability is very much a watchword at the moment, and so it should be. There are a few good organisations with websites and apps for your phone that will enable you to keep up to date with the constantly changing news about sustainable species (try www.msc.org and www.fishonline.org), but the best way to find out if your seafood is sustainable is to ask your fishmonger. He or she should be able to tell you everything about the seafood you are buying, notably whether it is sustainable and what fishing practice has been used to catch it. If they can't, go somewhere they can!

Understanding seasonality is important too. When fish and shellfish are spawning, we should avoid catching and eating them, to give them a chance to reproduce, thus encouraging the species to thrive. Recently spawned fish isn't good to eat anyway because all its energy has been used to create healthy eggs, so the quality of the muscle flesh is reduced. If we want to be able to choose from a variety of seafood in the future, we really cannot afford to overlook the issue of sustainability. So I urge you to ask before you buy and if you don't like what you hear, don't buy it.

Any fishmonger worth his or her salt will make sure you walk away with really great seafood. It's in their interest to do so. The whole seafood business is built up on trust; it's quite simple, if you don't get good service and fantastic fish you won't go back. The first thing you need to look for is cleanliness: clean fish (especially shellfish), clean display area, clean floor and clean fishmonger! A good fishmonger will want to show off his or her seafood proudly rather than hide it.

Next, take a closer look at the fish. Is there any visible damage? Where there should be scales, are they intact? Are the eyes clear, with almost a sparkle to them? Are the gills bright red, not dull? Check that there are no red bruise marks on the fish as this could be down to poor handling. Some fish, especially lemon sole and turbot, should have a nice layer of slime. And, as

I've said before, it should have that lovely smell of the sea that reminds you where it's come from, not an aroma that repels you.

Another tip. When you go to buy seafood, take a cool bag and ice blocks with you, unless you know your fishmonger will be packing the fish in ice when you buy it. Online fishmongers will use special packaging to ensure their seafood reaches you in good condition. When you get your fish home, I suggest you move your salad out of the salad drawer and use it for your fish instead.

Oysters and shellfish are ok stored at standard fridge temperature (4°C), but fish should, ideally, be kept at about 1°C (though a little higher won't hurt). You can achieve this by using ice packs, but don't place them in direct contact with the fish, or it will suffer freezer-burn. You'll also need to change the ice regularly, before it turns to water – sea fish do not take well to being kept in fresh water.

Fish freezes well and it's a sensible thing to do if you get the chance of a true bargain or are offered a large haul. Make sure it is very fresh though, then wrap it really well in freezer wrap, seal it in a bag and it will be fine for a few months. The best way to defrost fish is slowly in the fridge – either overnight or throughout the day if you are cooking it in the evening. Cooked lobster and crab also freeze well, if well wrapped.

When assembling your fish and seafood prep toolkit, the first item on your list should be a good-quality flexible filleting knife (but not one that is too bendable or it will be hard to control and potentially dangerous, not to mention difficult to sharpen). You'll also need a good heavy cook's knife for cracking lobsters and

cutting through the bones of fish for steaks. For the latter, I use a rubber mallet to hit the knife for extra force if necessary. When it comes to removing heads from whole fish, a strong, serrated knife is the ideal tool.

I use a sturdy boning knife to open scallop shells and to remove the flat shell, then I prise the scallop from the shell with a cheap, flat metal tablespoon (the sort you find in a school canteen or motorway service station). I also use the handle end of that spoon to pick out crab meat from the shell and lobster claws and knuckles.

For descaling fish, I find that a small, serrated knife is the easiest tool to use, but you can buy a proper fish descaler, or scrape away the scales with the edge of a scallop shell, if you prefer. Strong tweezers are essential for removing the pin bones from fish too.

Buy yourself a smooth, heavy, blue plastic chopping board and keep it solely for prepping fish. Generally, I don't favour plastic chopping boards, but with seafood it really is the only way. After use, wash it in cold water first to get rid of any fishy bits and then use hot, soapy water to wash it thoroughly. On really hot days I put the board in the fridge before I prepare my fish; it helps to keep the temperature down.

Of course, there are specific items of equipment for different cooking techniques and you'll find details of these at the start of each chapter. Please, don't skimp on quality. Good-quality equipment will last you a lifetime and it is much nicer to use. Cheaper alternatives are a false economy.

So, that's about it. You have some useful 'insider' tips, your fish and seafood toolkit is ready and all you need to do now is choose your recipe. Happy cooking!

This is where we start: no heat required, just the freshest and best quality seafood. Raw fish is a relatively new thing in the West, yet the Japanese have been eating sushi and sashimi for centuries. That's why I follow their lead in the knowledge of raw seafood, including the best varieties to use. Other cultures – Nordic, Italian, Spanish, South American and Caribbean – also have raw fish as part of their traditional diet but, to me, the Japanese are the masters.

Nearly all of our sea friends are edible, but not all of them are edible raw. So which fish are best for raw dishes? Well, for me, scallops, salmon and mackerel, as these are my favourites. Tuna, obviously, is great too, but we really only see our fisherman land albacore tuna, which is different from the tuna you usually find in sushi restaurants – typically yellowfin that has been fished in other oceans. Mind you, saying that, it is also nice prepared raw, just different.

The way fish and shellfish have been caught and kept from that point are vital considerations if you are eating them raw. Obviously, fishermen that supply the finest, freshest fish are your best source of supply. Their fish will have been killed swiftly, gutted quickly and bled well. It all sounds a little nasty, but it is essential that it is done this way. If the fish isn't killed swiftly it will become stressed and physiological reactions to stress have an adverse affect on the texture of the fish, causing it to become tough. If the fish isn't gutted quickly, any parasites will immediately try to attack and travel into the flesh from the guts. And if the fish isn't bled briskly, the blood will settle in the flesh, giving a very bitter taste and an unpleasant appearance.

RAW

It may well surprise you to learn that I usually prefer to freeze very fresh fish for raw preparations, except oysters. In most cases, freezing helps to tenderise the seafood, but its main purpose is to deal with parasites. I don't want to put you off, but parasites are everywhere – they're part of life – though freezing kills most of them. Many of the best sushi chefs in the world freeze their seafood and I'd recommend you do too, to be on the safe side.

I have eaten raw fish in restaurants in various countries and, of course, I serve it in my own. Of the dishes I have tasted, a few stand out for me: a razor clam dish at Noma in Copenhagen; an Italian raw prawn dish at The Seahorse in Dartmouth, Devon; and an oyster dish with pear at Mirazur in Menton, South of France. They all had one thing in common: simplicity.

In raw seafood dishes, more than any other preparation, simplicity is so important. Don't let raw fish scare you. It is fantastic, healthy and unique in flavour. Just be smart about where you get the fish, how you store it and what you put it with. Hopefully I can help you with that.

BEST FISH FOR RAW PREPARATION
Scallops, salmon, mackerel, horse mackerel, tuna, sea trout, brill, bream, bass, prawns, oysters, mussels, clams.

ACCOMPANIMENTS & GARNISHES
Citrus fruits, fresh herbs, vinegars, oils, pickled vegetables (page 216), vegetable marmalades (pages 45 and 58).

Raw bass with anchovy, mint and coriander dressing

At our fine dining restaurant we start the meal with a couple of raw and cured dishes, and my head chef Chris Simpson came up with this great combination. The dressing is versatile and can be used with lots of different fish, raw or cooked; it's especially good with pan-fried squid. The flavours are very fresh and you can chop and change the herbs if you like.

Serves 6 as a starter
1 bass, about 2kg, scaled and gutted
36 anchovy fillets in oil, drained
1 garlic clove, peeled and finely chopped
Finely grated zest of 1 lemon
1 tsp chopped flat-leaf parsley
About 50ml light rapeseed oil

Anchovy, mint and coriander dressing
3 anchovy fillets in oil, drained
25ml lime juice
50g coriander leaves
50g mint leaves
About 150ml light rapeseed oil
Cornish sea salt

Fillet and skin the bass (see pages 192–4), then freeze overnight.

Put the 36 anchovy fillets into a bowl or jar, sprinkle over the garlic, lemon zest and parsley and then drizzle with the rapeseed oil. Leave to marinate for at least 2 hours. (You can prepare the anchovies to this stage, cover and leave them to marinate for up to 3 days if you wish.)

Allow the bass to thaw slightly until you can slice it, then slice very thinly.

For the dressing, put the 3 anchovy fillets into a small food processor with the lime juice, coriander and mint, and blend for 1 minute. With the motor running, gradually add enough rapeseed oil to give the consistency of a thick pesto dressing. Season with salt to taste.

Lay the bass slices out on a large plate, season lightly with salt and arrange the marinated anchovies on top. Dress the fish with the herb and anchovy dressing and leave to stand for 30 minutes before serving.

Raw brill with rapeseed oil, orange and tarragon

This is probably the most straightforward dish in the book, but for me it is a fine example of treating the freshest and best quality fish very simply to appreciate its qualities to the full. You need to hone your knife skills to get the fish nice and thin, though if you cut it into small cubes it will work equally well. Orange and tarragon are a lovely combination and work extremely well with raw fish. When blood oranges are in season, do use them – the dish looks even more stunning!

<u>Serves 6 as a starter</u>
1 brill, about 2kg
2 oranges
Handful of fine tarragon leaves
100ml cold-pressed extra virgin rapeseed oil
Cornish sea salt

Fillet and skin the brill (see pages 185–6), then freeze overnight.

Allow the brill to thaw slightly until you can slice it, then slice it as thinly as possible. Lay the fish slices out evenly on large serving plates and season with sea salt.

Peel and segment the oranges, removing all the pith and membrane, then cut into small pieces.

Distribute the orange and tarragon evenly over the plates. Drizzle with the rapeseed oil and season with salt. Serve at room temperature.

Raw wild bream with horseradish, shallot and carrot pickle

Wild bream is such a lovely fish and it has a nice rich, yet refreshing, flavour when raw. The accompanying pickle works really well with it, I think. It's not a traditional pickle as such, but one that has the anticipated acidity and heat and retains a mighty crunch with the carrot and samphire.

<u>Serves 4 as a starter</u>
1 wild gilthead bream, 600g–800g
<u>Horseradish, shallot and carrot pickle</u>
A drizzle of light rapeseed oil
2 banana shallots, peeled and finely sliced
3 carrots, peeled and cut into fine ribbons
  (using a peeler or mandoline)
50g caster sugar
50ml white wine vinegar
4 tsp creamed horseradish
2 tsp chopped flat-leaf parsley
150g samphire
About 150ml cold-pressed extra virgin rapeseed oil
Cornish sea salt

Fillet and skin the bream (see pages 192–4), checking carefully for pin bones and removing any tough sinews, then freeze overnight.

To make the pickle, place a frying pan over a medium heat and add a drizzle of rapeseed oil. When the oil is hot, add the shallots and cook for 2 minutes until they are soft but not coloured. Add the carrots, sugar and wine vinegar and simmer for 1 minute. Now add the creamed horseradish and heat for another minute. Season with salt to taste, tip onto a tray and leave to cool.

When the pickle is cold, add the chopped parsley. Blanch the samphire in boiling salted water for 30 seconds, then refresh in ice-cold water and drain thoroughly once it is cold.

Mix half of the samphire through the pickle, then tip the mixture into a colander set over a bowl to collect the juice.

Thaw the bream slightly until you can slice it, then using a very sharp knife, cut it into very thin slices, 2–3mm thick.

Lay the bream out on individual plates or on one large plate and season with salt. Place a spoonful of pickle on each plate.

For the dressing, mix the collected pickle juice with the extra virgin rapeseed oil. Taste for seasoning, adding a little salt if needed.

Spoon some of the dressing over the fish and scatter over the rest of the samphire. Serve the rest of the dressing in a jug on the side for everyone to help themselves.

Scallops tartare
'tartare'

This dish marries some of my favourite flavours from the classic tartare sauce with raw scallops, hence the name. Here, you really do need scallops cut from the shell live. In fact, I find it's the best way to use them when they are that fresh, as they are too firm for pan-frying or grilling for the first day or so.

Serves 4 as a starter
12 large live scallops in the shell
½ lemon
1 tsp finely chopped chives
1 tsp finely chopped flat-leaf parsley
1 tsp finely chopped chervil
1 tsp finely chopped tarragon
Cornish sea salt and freshly ground black pepper

Tartare sauce
1 spring onion, trimmed and finely sliced
2 tsp finely chopped gherkins
2 tsp capers in brine, drained and chopped
1 tsp finely chopped chives
1 tsp finely chopped flat-leaf parsley
1 tsp finely chopped chervil
1 tsp finely chopped tarragon
3 egg yolks
Juice of ½ lemon
1 tsp English mustard
300ml light rapeseed oil, plus extra to drizzle

To serve
1 salad or spring onion, trimmed and finely sliced
   into rings
Lemon wedges

Shell and clean the scallops (see pages 206–7), removing the roes, then freeze overnight.

For the tartare sauce, combine the spring onion, gherkins, capers and chopped herbs in a small bowl. Put the egg yolks, lemon juice and mustard into a separate medium bowl and whisk together for 1 minute. Slowly whisk in the rapeseed oil to emulsify and thicken the mayonnaise. Stir in the tartare mixture and season with salt and pepper to taste. Cover and refrigerate until ready to serve.

Thaw the scallops until you can slice them, then cut into 5mm dice. Segment the lemon half, removing all pith and membrane, to give half segments.

In a clean bowl, combine the scallops, half lemon segments and herbs. Add a couple of spoonfuls of the tartare sauce and mix well. Taste for seasoning and add salt and pepper as required.

To serve, arrange the scallop tartare mixture on individual plates. Spoon on some of the tartare sauce and drizzle with a little rapeseed oil. Scatter the onion rings over the top.

Serve with lemon wedges, and the rest of the tartare sauce in a bowl on the side.

Raw queenie scallops, tomato water dressing and crisp-fried queenies

When tomatoes are at their best we use them in lots of different ways. Tomato water is a really great way to use a glut of tomatoes. Its intense flavour and acidity work so well with raw fish, queen scallops in particular. We buy our queenies from the Isle of Man – they're a fantastic ingredient and very versatile. This is a fine dish to kick off a summer's day lunch.

Serves 4 as a starter

24 queenie scallops, or 12 standard (king) scallops
1kg very ripe flavourful plum tomatoes
12 ripe cherry (or baby plum) tomatoes
50ml light rapeseed oil
2 tsp chopped chives
Oil for deep-frying

Batter

50g strong plain flour, plus a little extra to dust
50g cornflour
100ml ice-cold soda water
Cornish sea salt

Shell and clean the scallops if necessary (see pages 206–7), removing the roes. Quickly rinse the scallops, making sure they are free from sand and any bits of skirt. Freeze overnight.

For the tomato water, blitz the plum tomatoes in a food processor with a good pinch of salt to a purée. Lay a large square of muslin or a clean tea towel over a medium bowl, allowing the ends to drape over the sides. Tip the puréed tomatoes into the muslin. Gather the ends of the muslin over the top and tie into a bag with string, then suspend over the bowl. Leave in the fridge overnight to allow the tomato water to drip through. If you haven't time for that, you could just give it a squeeze to extract the liquid.

Thaw the scallops. Set aside 12 queenies or 6 king scallops (slicing the latter in half). Carefully slice the rest of the scallops across in half and lay the scallop discs out on a tray. Refrigerate, unless serving straight away.

To make the batter, mix the flour and cornflour together in a bowl and whisk in the soda water, then season with a good pinch of salt.

Just before serving, slice the cherry tomatoes. Arrange the sliced scallops and tomato slices on individual plates, overlapping them neatly.

For the dressing, measure 180ml of the tomato water and whisk with the rapeseed oil. Season with salt. Dress each plate with the tomato dressing and sprinkle over the chopped chives.

Heat the oil in a deep-fat fryer to 180°C. Roll the remaining scallops through a little flour, shaking off any excess. Dip them, one at a time, into the batter to coat, then lower into the hot oil. Deep-fry for about 1 minute until golden and crispy. Remove with a slotted spoon, drain on kitchen paper and season with salt.

Place the hot, crispy scallops on the plates and serve at once.

Raw oysters, cucumber jelly and dill cream

This dish is a fantastic starter for a special occasion meal, because the presentation is a real show-piece. To me, oysters smell a bit like cucumber, so it makes sense to pair them. Here, the touch of dill and horseradish gives them a lift and a little bit of oomph! Source your oysters carefully – they must be very fresh, especially when you're eating them raw.

Serves 4 as a starter
15 live oysters
1 cucumber
20ml white wine vinegar
15g caster sugar
4 sheets of bronze leaf gelatine (4g each)
200ml double cream
30g good-quality creamed horseradish
2 tbsp chopped dill
Dill or fennel fronds to finish
Seaweed to serve (optional)

Open the oysters (see page 204) and strain off their juice through a muslin-lined sieve into a bowl. Wash and reserve 12 shells. Carefully rinse each oyster in the strained juice, then place on a clean tray. Trim if necessary, then cover and chill until required.

Roughly chop the cucumber and put it into a blender with the wine vinegar, sugar and 3 oysters. Strain the oyster juice again and add it to the blender. Blitz for 1 minute, then strain the liquid through a muslin-lined sieve. Measure out 200ml; reserve the rest.

Soak 2 gelatine leaves in a shallow dish of cold water. Meanwhile, heat 50ml of the measured liquid (until hot but not boiling), then take off the heat. Drain the gelatine and squeeze out excess water, then add to the warm liquid, stirring to dissolve. Stir in the rest of the measured liquid and set this molten jelly aside.

Measure another 100ml of the oyster and cucumber liquid into a pan, add the cream and horseradish and whisk together. Soak the remaining 2 gelatine leaves in cold water. Heat the cream mixture, until hot enough to dissolve the gelatine, then add the gelatine and whisk to dissolve. Strain through a sieve into a jug.

Lay out the oyster shells on something to keep the shells level and straight (I use a large egg box but you could use a muffin tray).

Stir the chopped dill into the cream. Carefully pour the cream mixture into the oyster shells, dividing it equally, and place in the fridge to set for 1 hour.

Once the cream has set, add an oyster to each shell and spoon on the molten jelly to cover. Put back in the fridge to set; this should take less than 30 minutes.

To serve, arrange the oysters on a bed of seaweed (or pebbles) on a large serving platter or individual plates and garnish with feathery dill or fennel fronds.

The term 'cured' is generally applied to fish that has been fermented, pickled or smoked to preserve it, but in my kitchen it describes fish that has been cured in a wet or dry salt cure mixture. (We think of fermenting, pickling and smoking as processes that we can apply to our cured fish.) Our aim isn't for an extended shelf life, although of course that is an advantage. For me, it's the change in texture that is magical and makes our cured dishes unique.

Salting is an effective way of preserving food because it draws out moisture and inhibits the action of bacteria and other potentially harmful micro-organisms, which are unable to function in a salty environment. Table salt is commonly employed for curing but we use Cornish sea salt or rock salt because I think you can taste the anti-caking agents in table salt on the finished cured product. Nitrates are also used in industrial food curing to prevent botulism in fish and help to kill bacteria; they also give the fish a pinkish colour. As we are not producing for the mass market we don't need nitrates – we just stick to the salt!

There are, however, a few traditional cured fish that I buy – notably salt cod, salt herring and tinned anchovies – as they are convenient standby ingredients.

The earliest of the curing techniques – dehydration, salt cure and smoking – date back as far as 3000 BC. The Greeks are thought to have been the first to produce salt in a farmed way. They would use their salt to cure meats and fish, then trade with the resulting cured products. The Romans moved the salting process on

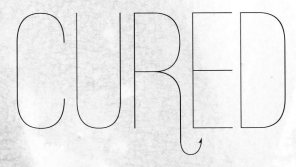

CURED

further, pickling meat and fish using brines. Interestingly, the term 'cure' comes from the Latin *curare*, which means to take care of. I quite like that! Maybe I'll write it like that on my menus: 'Bream that has been taken care of' has a certain charm.

And we do take care over curing our fish, often flavouring the salt with citrus zests and selected spices, as well as sugar or sometimes honey, to balance out the flavour so the salt isn't as harsh.

Curing also allows us to make some of the less flavourful species taste special – by reducing the water content, which intensifies the flavour, and enhancing the cure with other flavourings. For example, pouting and coley are relatively bland fish but a salt cure flavoured with citrus zests takes them to another level. In general, I find the oilier fish tend to be better for

curing, but the whiter varieties seem to take on more of the additional flavours.

Currently, my favourite fish to cure are bream, mackerel and the cod family, but we are constantly developing new cured dishes and these could change tomorrow! That's why I love curing: the adventure is endless.

BEST FISH FOR CURING
Bream, mackerel, pollack, ling, hake, bass, brill, sea trout, salmon, cod, coley, grey mullet, haddock, farmed halibut, herring, pouting, prawns, horse mackerel, sardines, sprat, trout, whiting.

ACCOMPANIMENTS & GARNISHES
Pickled vegetables (page 216), vegetable marmalades (pages 45 and 58), citrus fruits, herbs, vinegars, oils, mustards, horseradish.

Cured brill with mint and peas

Brill isn't a fish one would generally expect to find cured, but while experimenting as I do (though not always with great success), I discovered that it was really well suited. Usually much oilier fish fit the bill, but in this minty cure brill is perfect. It goes without saying that peas and mint pair well and here they team beautifully with the cured fish.

Serves 4
500g brill fillet, skinned and trimmed
400g freshly podded peas

Cure
100g sea salt
100g caster sugar
40g mint leaves
70ml water

Dressing
100ml cold-pressed rapeseed oil
40ml cider vinegar
5g mint leaves, chopped
Cornish sea salt

To finish
A few mint sprigs
Handful of pea shoots or tendrils

For the cure, put the sea salt, sugar, mint and water in a food processor and blitz together for 1 minute.

Lay the brill fillet on a tray and pour the salt cure over it. Make sure the fish is evenly coated all over. Cover with cling film and leave to cure in the fridge for 2½ hours.

Now wash off the cure well with cold water and pat the fish dry with kitchen paper. Wrap the fish tightly in cling film and place in the fridge for an hour or so. (At this stage, you can freeze the fish for up to a month.)

Add the peas to a pan of boiling water and blanch for a minute or two until just tender. Drain and refresh under cold water; drain well.

For the dressing, whisk the rapeseed oil and cider vinegar together, add the chopped mint and season with salt to taste.

Unwrap the brill. Using a very sharp knife, slice the fish on a clean board as thinly as possible, laying it straight onto serving plates. Spoon the dressing evenly over the fish and sprinkle with a little salt. Scatter over the peas and finish with the mint sprigs and pea shoots.

Cured wild bream with fennel, citrus fruit and pastis soured cream

Wild black or gilthead bream is fantastic when cured. Its flesh has a slightly oily quality that responds particularly well to the curing process. I've done it so many ways, but this is my favourite (well, for now anyway!). The citrus and fennel go so well together with the bream. I've also made this successfully with grey mullet and bass.

Serves 4
2 wild black or gilthead bream, about 500g each, filleted, skinned, pin-boned and trimmed (see pages 192–4)

Cure
Finely grated zest of 2 lemons
Finely grated zest of 2 limes
250g sea salt
500g caster sugar
25g honey
5g fennel seeds
10 tarragon sprigs
100ml pastis

Fennel and citrus fruit
1 fennel bulb, trimmed, feathery fronds reserved
1 orange
1 lemon
1 pink grapefruit
2 fennel herb or dill sprigs, chopped
100ml cold-pressed rapeseed oil
Cornish sea salt and freshly ground black pepper

Pastis soured cream
250ml soured cream
2 tbsp pastis

For the cure, put the lemon and lime zest, sea salt, sugar, honey, fennel seeds, tarragon sprigs and pastis in a bowl and mix together well.

Lay the bream fillets on a tray (that will hold both the fish and cure) and pour the cure over them, making sure it is evenly distributed and the fish is covered all over. Cover with cling film and leave to cure in the fridge for 2 hours.

Wash off the cure well with cold water, pat the fish dry with kitchen paper, then wrap tightly in cling film and place back in the fridge for an hour or so. (At this stage, you can freeze the fish for up to a month.)

To prepare the fennel, remove any tough outer layer, then slice very finely, using a mandoline if you have one. Immerse in ice-cold water for 20 minutes to firm and crisp the slices.

For the pastis soured cream, whip the cream with the pastis until it is firm, then cover and refrigerate until ready to use.

Peel and segment the orange, lemon and pink grapefruit, removing all of the white pith and membrane, then cut into small pieces and place in a bowl with the chopped fennel herb (or dill) and the rapeseed oil. Turn to coat in the dressing and season with salt to taste; put to one side.

To serve, carefully slice the bream. Drain the citrus fruit and set aside, reserving the dressing.

Drain the fennel and give it a good shake in the colander to remove excess water. Add the fennel to the reserved dressing, mix well and season with salt and pepper to taste.

Lay the cured fish neatly on individual plates or a large sharing plate and top with the citrus fruit. Place a nice pile of fennel alongside and garnish with the feathery fronds. Spoon the pastis cream around to serve.

Whisky cured salmon with kohlrabi and horseradish yoghurt

The first time I cured salmon with whisky was at my first restaurant, The Black Pig. It's a recipe I always come back to. Whisky, horseradish and saffron might sound like a clashing combination but it works brilliantly with the salmon, which has such a strong flavour that it remains the star of the show.

Serves 10

1 side of wild or organic farmed salmon, about 1.5kg, skinned, pin-boned and trimmed

Cure
250g sea salt
250g caster sugar
150ml whisky

Pickled kohlrabi
1 large kohlrabi
100ml olive oil
70ml light rapeseed oil
50ml white wine vinegar
1 large banana shallot, peeled and finely chopped
Pinch of saffron strands

Horseradish yoghurt
200ml Greek yoghurt
2 tsp creamed horseradish
Cornish sea salt and freshly ground black pepper

To finish
Finely sliced flat-leaf parsley

To cure the salmon, lay it on a tray and sprinkle the salt, sugar and whisky over evenly, making sure the fish is covered all over. Cover with cling film and place in the fridge for 12 hours.

Peel the kohlrabi and slice very thinly, using a mandoline if you have one. Put the olive and rapeseed oils, wine vinegar and shallot into a saucepan with the saffron and a pinch of salt, and bring to a simmer over a medium heat. Lay the kohlrabi slices in a dish and pour over the simmering liquid, making sure the slices are submerged. Cover with cling film and leave to cool, then refrigerate until required.

To make the horseradish yoghurt, mix the yoghurt and horseradish together in a bowl and season with salt and pepper to taste. Cover and keep in the fridge until required.

Wash off the salt mixture well from the cured salmon with cold water and pat dry with kitchen paper. Cover tightly with cling film and return to the fridge for an hour or so to firm up.

When ready to serve, drain off most of the liquor from the kohlrabi into another bowl, adding some of the chopped shallot too. Set aside for the dressing.

Finely slice the salmon into 3mm thick pieces and arrange on a platter with the pickled kohlrabi. Allow to come to room temperature.

Dress the salmon and plates with the shallot dressing and finish with a scattering of sliced parsley. Serve the chilled horseradish yoghurt in a bowl on the side.

Paprika cured grey mullet, pickled peppers and saffron potato salad

Grey mullet has a unique flavour and a distinctive texture that are beautifully enhanced when cured with smoked paprika. Pickled peppers and a salad of waxy potatoes infused with saffron are the perfect partners.

Serves 4
1 grey mullet, about 1.5kg, filleted, skinned and pin-boned (see pages 192–4)
150ml olive oil
Cornish sea salt and freshly ground black pepper

Cure
75g sea salt
75g caster sugar
20g smoked paprika

Pickled peppers
1 yellow pepper
1 green pepper
1 red pepper
A little olive oil for cooking
1 shallot, peeled and finely sliced
2 garlic cloves, peeled and crushed
2 bay leaves
75g caster sugar
75ml white wine
75ml white wine vinegar
75ml water
1 tsp chopped coriander
1 tsp chopped mint

Saffron potato salad
200g waxy potatoes, peeled
½ tsp saffron strands
2 spring onions, shredded
1 tsp chopped mint
1 tsp chopped coriander
Pinch of smoked paprika

For the cure, mix together the salt, sugar and smoked paprika. Lay the fish fillets on a tray, scatter over the cure and turn the fish to coat all over with the paprika salt mix. Cover with cling film and place in the fridge to cure for 8 hours.

Wash off the cure well with cold water and pat the fish dry with kitchen paper. Wrap the fish tightly in cling film and place back in the fridge for an hour or so. (At this stage, you can freeze the fish for up to a month.)

To prepare the pickled peppers, peel, halve and core the peppers, then slice them thinly. Heat a frying pan with a drizzle of olive oil. When hot, add the sliced peppers, shallot, garlic and bay leaves and cook over a medium heat for 4 minutes, stirring occasionally. Now add the sugar, wine, wine vinegar and water and simmer for 2 minutes, then remove from the heat. Season with salt to taste and allow to cool.

To make the potato salad, cut the potatoes into wedges and add to a saucepan of cold water with the saffron and some salt. Bring to a simmer and cook for 15 minutes or until the potatoes are tender. Drain the potatoes and allow them to cool slightly.

Drain the pickled peppers, reserving the liquor. Toss the peppers with the coriander and mint.

Unwrap and slice the cured fish.

For the dressing, mix 100ml of the reserved pickling liquor with the olive oil. Dress the fish with some of the dressing, saving the rest.

Toss the warm potatoes with the shredded spring onions, mint and coriander, then season with salt and pepper to taste. Transfer to a serving plate and finish with a sprinkling of smoked paprika.

Arrange the fish and pickled peppers on a platter and add a touch more dressing. Serve the saffron potato salad on the side.

Mackerel cured in cucumber and oyster juice with cucumber, dill and caper salad

This recipe was invented by accident. Someone had forgotten to cover the oyster juice in the fridge and as the door shut it toppled over onto my beautifully prepared mackerel fillets. I came into work to find the mess... and my mackerel swimming in oyster juice! I may have uttered a few expletives at the time, but soon discovered that the fish was, in fact, not ruined but delicious. Instantly I set about creating this dish. Whoever it was in my kitchen who slammed that fridge door never owned up so I can't credit them, but this recipe is dedicated to them anyway!

Serves 4
4 mackerel, filleted, skinned and pin-boned
　(see pages 192–4)
Cure
1 cucumber, roughly chopped
200g sea salt
100g caster sugar
10g dill
6 oysters, shucked, juice strained and reserved
　(see page 204)
Cucumber, dill and caper salad
1 cucumber
3 tsp small capers in brine, drained
2 tsp white wine shallots (see page 216)
2 tsp chopped dill, plus extra sprigs to finish
4 tsp lemon juice
8 tsp cold-pressed rapeseed oil
Cornish sea salt and freshly ground black pepper

For the cure, put the cucumber, salt, sugar and dill in a food processor with the oysters and their juice and blitz for 1 minute.

Lay the mackerel fillets on a tray (that will hold them and the cure) and pour the cure over them, distributing it evenly and making sure the fillets are covered all over. Cover with cling film and place in the fridge to cure for 2 hours.

Wash off the cure well with cold water and pat the fish dry with kitchen paper. Wrap the fish tightly in cling film and place in the fridge for an hour or so. (At this stage, you can freeze the fish for up to a month.)

In the meantime, prepare the salad. Peel the cucumber, then pare long ribbons from the sides, using a vegetable peeler, until you reach the seeds, then stop. Put the cucumber ribbons into a bowl with the capers, white wine shallots and chopped dill.

Preheat your grill to medium. Unwrap the cured mackerel fillets and grill them skin side up for 2 minutes, then remove and break into flakes. Gently toss the mackerel with the cucumber salad. Dress with the lemon juice and rapeseed oil and season with salt and pepper to taste. Finish with a scattering of dill sprigs.

Serve either as a sharing dish in the centre of the table or on individual plates.

Sea trout cured in seaweed and cider with pickled shimeji and mushroom cream

Sea trout is such a versatile fish and the slight fattiness of its flesh makes it ideal for curing. It's also very forgiving if you leave it in the cure for too long. And don't worry if you're curing more than you need – it freezes well too. Of all the cured recipes, this is the one that shows the technique in its best light, so please do give it a try.

Serves 8 generously

1 side of wild sea trout, about 2kg, skinned, pin-boned and trimmed

Cure

200g sea salt
200g caster sugar
2 sharp eating apples, quartered
6 tsp dried seaweed flakes
150ml cider

Mushroom cream

A little light rapeseed oil for cooking
1 white onion, peeled and chopped
325g button mushrooms, sliced
200ml double cream
Juice of 1 lime

Pickled shimeji

2 tbsp light rapeseed oil
2 banana shallots, peeled and finely chopped
500g shimeji mushrooms
75ml cider vinegar

To assemble

2 tart eating apples
6 tsp dried seaweed flakes, plus 1 tsp to finish
70ml cold-pressed rapeseed oil
Handful of tarragon leaves

For the cure, put the salt, sugar, apples, seaweed flakes and cider in a food processor and blitz together for 1 minute.

Lay the prepared sea trout in a tray (that will hold both the fish and cure). Pour the cure over the sea trout, making sure it is evenly distributed and the fish is covered all over. Cover with cling film and place in the fridge to cure for 12 hours.

Wash off the cure well with cold water and pat the fish dry with kitchen paper. Wrap the fish tightly in cling film and keep in the fridge (for up to 4 days) until ready to serve. (At this stage, you can freeze the fish for up to a month.).

For the mushroom cream, heat a large saucepan with a little oil. Add the onion and cook for 1 minute, then add the mushrooms. Cook over a medium heat until the mushrooms have released their liquid and started to colour, about 15 minutes. Add the cream and season with salt and pepper. Bring to the boil and then take off the heat. Tip into a blender, add the lime juice and blend until smooth. Pour into a bowl and allow to cool, then cover and refrigerate.

For the pickled shimeji, heat a frying pan over a medium heat with the oil. Add the shallots and cook for 1 minute until soft but not coloured, then add the shimeji mushrooms and cook for 2 minutes. Now pour in the cider vinegar, season with salt to taste and take off the heat. Tip the mushrooms onto a tray and allow to cool.

To serve, dice the sea trout and place in a large bowl. Peel and dice the apples and add to the cured fish with the shimeji mushrooms, seaweed and rapeseed oil. Toss gently to mix.

Share the mixture between 4 plates and spoon a generous dollop of the mushroom cream to one side. Scatter a pinch of seaweed flakes and some tarragon leaves over each portion to finish.

My first encounter with pickled seafood was on Hastings seafront in East Sussex with my dad and granddad. All along the Old Town there were stalls selling pickled cockles amongst other seaside classics like rollmops, jellied eels, pints of shrimps and prawns and those god-awful crab sticks. The pleasure of sitting there, watching the waves and listening to the seagulls whilst eating our pickled cockles, is one of my earliest and fondest childhood memories.

For centuries, pickling and sousing have been used as ways of preserving fish. Probably the oldest and most common sousing is found in the classic soused herring, which dates back to the Middle Ages – in Dutch, German and Swedish culinary traditions as well as ours. The best time for sousing herring is from the end of May to early July, when the fish are rich with oils and haven't yet started to develop their prized milts (roe). Jars of rollmops – which are simply rolled soused herring – are a British tradition.

Fish is well suited to pickling and sousing. Whether it's in a light sousing vinegar or a heavy pickling one, the acidity always seems to work well with the fish. Shellfish too – particularly scallops, oysters and lobster – can be enhanced beautifully with a light pickling liquor.

So how do pickling and sousing differ? Well, for pickling, the fish are immersed in a cold acidic liquid (usually wine vinegar), with spices and/or other aromatics added. Sousing is similar, but vegetables are added to the pickling liquor and it is added hot to the fish. It goes without saying, but I will say it: always use the freshest fish and shellfish for these techniques.

PICKLED & SOUSED

What I like most about these techniques is the scope they offer for experimenting. By using different vinegars (or other acidic liquids) and varying the herbs, spices and vegetables, you really can create your own take on pickled fish.

Herrings are my favourite fish to pickle – you'll find the recipe in my first book, *Nathan Outlaw's British Seafood*.

The way I like to souse fish is to take something like mackerel (my firm favourite) and fillet it nicely, making sure all the pin bones are taken out. I slice a red onion and sweat it in a little olive oil with some garlic, bay leaves and thyme for a few minutes, then add some cider vinegar, a pinch of sugar and some dry cider and simmer it for a couple of minutes before pouring it over the mackerel. I leave it in the fridge for a day, taking it out half an hour or so before needed, to bring it to room temperature. Before eating, I warm it slightly under the grill and serve it with a fresh apple and horseradish yoghurt. Delicious.

BEST SEAFOOD FOR PICKLING & SOUSING
Scallops, mackerel, horse mackerel, herring, sea trout, bream, bass, prawns, salmon, farmed halibut, clams, cockles, oysters, grey mullet, gurnard, mussels, lobster, red mullet, razor clams, sardines.

ACCOMPANIMENTS & GARNISHES
Horseradish yoghurt (page 35), fennel marmalade (page 58), beetroot chutney, cucumber, dill and caper salad (page 38), potato and spring onion salad.

Pickled herring with red pepper marmalade and shellfish dressing

Of all the pickled herrings I have done, this is one of my favourites. We serve it as one of our first courses in the fine dining restaurant and it's the perfect dinner party dish. Everything is prepared beforehand, so all you have to remember is to remove it from the fridge an hour before the meal so that it is served at room temperature.

Serves 4

4 herrings, scaled, gutted, butterflied
    (see pages 196–7) and pin-boned
½ tsp coriander seeds
1 tsp black peppercorns
2 thyme sprigs
2 shallots, peeled and finely sliced
250ml cider vinegar
100g caster sugar
Cornish sea salt

Red pepper marmalade
3 red peppers
1 red onion, peeled and sliced
2 garlic cloves, peeled and chopped
100ml white wine vinegar
1 tsp chopped thyme
A little olive oil for cooking
40g caster sugar

Shellfish dressing
150ml shellfish stock (see page 213)
50ml cold-pressed rapeseed oil

To pickle the herrings, lay them in a dish large enough to hold them side by side submerged in the pickling liquor. Put the coriander seeds, peppercorns, thyme, shallots, cider vinegar and sugar into a small pan and bring to a simmer. Simmer for 2 minutes, then add 1 tsp of salt. Take off the heat and leave to cool.

Once cooled, pour the liquid and all the flavourings over the herrings and cover the fish closely with a layer of cling film to keep them submerged in the liquor. Place in the fridge and leave for 24 hours before eating.

To make the pepper marmalade, heat your oven to 200°C/Gas 6. Roast the peppers on a roasting tray in the oven for 30 minutes. Transfer to a bowl, cover with cling film and leave to cool: the trapped steam will help to lift the skins.

Meanwhile, put the red onion, garlic, wine vinegar and thyme into a pan and bring to a simmer. Let bubble over a medium heat until the liquid has reduced right down, almost to nothing; be careful not to burn the onions.

Peel the skins from the peppers, then halve, core, deseed and slice them thinly. Heat a large non-stick frying pan over a medium heat. When hot, add a drizzle of oil and then add the sliced peppers and sugar. Cook for 2 minutes, then add the red onion mixture. Cook until the juice has reduced to almost nothing. Taste and season the marmalade, allow to cool, then chill.

For the shellfish dressing, in a bowl, whisk the shellfish stock and rapeseed oil with a pinch of salt to combine thoroughly; set aside.

Drain the herring fillets. Lay half of them skin side down on a sheet of cling film. Spread each one with red pepper marmalade and place another fillet on top to make a sandwich.

Place a 'herring sandwich' on each plate and spoon on the shellfish dressing to serve.

Soused red mullet with saffron and carrots

Inspired by the classic escabeche, this is one way to get the very best from a red mullet. And, as a bonus, the fish passes its beautiful flavour to the saffrony sousing liquid, which lends a unique flavour to the dressing and carrots. A match made in heaven!

Serves 4
4 small red mullet, about 400g each, or 2 larger fish, scaled, filleted and pin-boned (see pages 192–4)
100ml light rapeseed oil, plus extra for cooking
1 shallot, peeled and diced
4 large carrots, peeled and cut into fine ribbons (using a peeler or mandoline)
75ml white wine vinegar
150ml olive oil
½ garlic clove, peeled
A good pinch of saffron strands

Carrot purée
A little light rapeseed oil for cooking
25g butter
500g carrots, peeled and roughly chopped
½ tsp ground cardamom
150ml water
Cornish sea salt and freshly ground black pepper

To finish
Carrot or coriander leaves

For the carrot purée, heat a drizzle of rapeseed oil in a medium saucepan and add the butter. Once melted, toss in the carrots with the cardamom and sweat for 3 minutes. Add the water, cover and cook over a medium-low heat, without colouring, until soft. Add a bit more water if they begin to stick. Once the carrots are soft, transfer them to a blender and blitz until smooth, adding a little of the cooking liquor to get a good consistency if need be. Season with salt and pepper to taste. Set aside for serving.

To souse the fish, heat a non-stick frying pan and add a drizzle of oil. When hot, fry the fillets skin side down for 30 seconds. Transfer to a dish large enough to hold them side by side submerged in the sousing liquor.

Add a touch more oil to the pan and place over a medium-low heat. Add the shallot and carrot ribbons and cook gently, without colouring, for 1 minute. Add the wine vinegar, 100ml rapeseed oil, olive oil, garlic and saffron and bring to a simmer. Season with salt to taste.

Pour the pickling mixture over the red mullet fillets. Cover with cling film so that the fish is held submerged under the liquor and leave for 1½ hours before serving. (Or, if serving the next day, allow to cool, then refrigerate.)

To serve, gently warm the carrot purée. Spoon the carrot ribbons onto plates, lay the soused red mullet on top and drizzle with a little of the oil from the sousing liquor. Spoon the carrot purée alongside. Garnish with carrot or coriander leaves.

Soused sardines with white cabbage and mustard

This dish has its roots in Eastern Europe. My head chef, Redas Katauskas from Lithuania, made a similar dish with herring, which inspired me to come up with this one. I've added a West Country twist with cider vinegar and apples and a touch of nostalgia with the salad cream. This dish would also work with herrings or fresh anchovies.

Serves 4

4 large or 8 small sardines, scaled, gutted, butterflied (see pages 196–7) and pin-boned
Light rapeseed oil for cooking and dressing
1 white onion, peeled and finely sliced
1 garlic clove, peeled and chopped
½ white cabbage, cored and finely shredded
200ml cider vinegar
100ml water
75g caster sugar
2 Braeburn apples
1 tbsp chopped tarragon
Cornish sea salt

Salad cream

2 egg yolks
2 tsp wholegrain mustard
2 tsp caster sugar
2 tbsp cider vinegar
200ml light rapeseed oil
50ml double cream

To souse the sardines, heat a non-stick frying pan and add a drizzle of rapeseed oil. When hot, add the sardines skin side down and fry for 1 minute until golden. Transfer the sardines to a dish large enough to hold them side by side submerged in the sousing liquor.

Add a touch more oil to the pan and return to a medium heat. When hot, add the onion, garlic and cabbage and cook, without colouring, until the cabbage starts to collapse. Add the cider vinegar, water and sugar to the pan and bring to the boil. Season with salt to taste. Tip the mixture over the sardines and leave at room temperature for 30 minutes before serving. (Or, if serving the next day, allow to cool, then refrigerate.)

To make the salad cream, put the egg yolks, mustard, sugar and cider vinegar in a bowl and whisk together for 1 minute. Now gradually add the oil, drop by drop to begin with, then in a steady stream, until it is all incorporated. To finish, slowly whisk in the cream and season with salt to taste. Refrigerate until required.

Drain the soused vegetables of their sousing liquor and place them in a large bowl. Halve, core, peel and shred the apples, then add to the vegetables with the chopped tarragon. Dress with a little rapeseed oil and taste for seasoning.

To serve, place the sardines on individual plates and add a portion of soused cabbage and onion. Finish with a good dollop of salad cream.

Lightly pickled lobster and leek kebabs

Every so often I have come up with an idea that my chefs think is odd – until they taste it! This is one of them. Unfortunately, and naturally, not all lobsters are landed in perfect condition. Sometimes one of the large claws is missing or they are too big to serve whole. This recipe is perfect, because it calls for nice chunks of meat. You could put whatever vegetable you want on these kebabs, but I like the char of leeks with the lobster and herbs. It's a perfect dish for a barbecue.

Serves 4
4 lobsters, 600–800g each
16 baby leeks, trimmed and washed
100ml white wine vinegar
Finely pared zest of 1 lemon, chopped
2 garlic cloves, peeled and finely chopped
100ml olive oil
Handful each of parsley, chives and mint
Cornish sea salt
Lime wedges to serve

Place the lobsters in the freezer for an hour before cooking to put them to sleep.

Bring a large pan of well-salted water to the boil. Add the leeks and simmer for 2 minutes. Remove the leeks with a slotted spoon, drain, cool and set aside (keep the boiling water).

Take the lobsters out of the freezer and place them on a board. To kill them instantly, firmly insert the tip of a strong, sharp knife through the cross on the head. Twist and pull off the heads, claws and legs. Blanch the tails in the boiling water (used for the leeks) for 2 minutes. Remove and drain. Add the claws to the pan and cook for 5 minutes. Carefully remove the meat from the tails and set aside. Drain the claws, crack them open and extract the meat.

To make the kebabs, you will need 8 short skewers. Cut the lobster tail into 2cm chunks and the claw meat into bite-sized pieces. Thread the tail meat, baby leeks and claw meat alternately onto the skewers. Lay the kebabs in a shallow dish.

For the dressing, combine the wine vinegar, lemon zest, garlic and olive oil in a bowl and mix well. Pour half of the dressing over the lobster kebabs, cover and leave to stand for 30 minutes.

Light the barbecue or heat a non-stick char-grill pan. Finely chop the herbs, add to the remaining dressing and stir to combine. When the barbecue or pan is hot, add the skewers and cook for 2 minutes on each side.

Serve the skewers immediately, with some of the dressing spooned over and lime wedges. Serve the rest of the herb dressing in a bowl on the side.

Lightly pickled oysters with gherkin, cucumber and jalapeño chilli

We have fantastic oysters on our doorstep and I'm always thinking of interesting ways to use them. Flavour-wise, they are powerful little things so don't be afraid to spice them up. Here, the freshness of cucumber and radish with the heat from the chilli work so well with the lightly pickled oysters. An ideal dish to scale up and serve to kick-off a party.

Serves 4 as a starter
12 live Pacific oysters
2 large gherkins, plus 100ml vinegar from the jar
1 jalapeño chilli
1 cucumber
1 large banana shallot, peeled and finely chopped
1 garlic clove, peeled and finely chopped
1 tbsp finely chopped dill
100ml light rapeseed oil
Seaweed to serve

Open the oysters (see page 204) and strain off their juice through a muslin-lined sieve into a small bowl.

Put the gherkin vinegar into a another bowl and add 100ml of the oyster juice. Add the shucked oysters, making sure they are fully submerged. Cover with cling film, and leave for 2 hours before serving. Wash the oyster shells thoroughly and reserve.

Slice the chilli into rounds, leaving the seeds in. Dice the cucumber and gherkins, or shape into balls using a melon baller, and place in a bowl. Add the chilli, shallot, garlic and dill and toss to combine.

To serve, lay the oyster shells on a bed of seaweed. Remove the oysters from their pickling liquor and place one in each shell.

For the dressing, mix the rapeseed oil with 4 tbsp of the oyster pickling liquor. Add a little pile of the gherkin and cucumber mixture to each oyster shell and spoon on the dressing.

Pickled scallops with red wine dressing and wild garlic oil

My head chef, Chris Simpson, and I enjoy an experiment now and again. This dish came about on a quieter winter's day when we had time to play around in the kitchen. We both love raw scallops and wanted to add acidity to them, but also colour them somehow. The result was really interesting – tasty and unique.

Serves 4
12 live scallops in the shell

Pickling liquor
200ml red wine
100ml water
50ml red wine vinegar
50g caster sugar
50g salt

Red wine reduction
100ml red wine vinegar
100ml water
100g caster sugar
100ml red wine

To serve
1 tbsp capers in brine, drained
1 tbsp chopped gherkins
1 tbsp chopped chives
Wild garlic oil (see page 214)
1 tbsp crispy fried capers (see page 217), optional

For the pickling liquor, put all the ingredients into a pan and bring to the boil, then remove from the heat and set aside to cool.

Shell and clean the scallops (see pages 206–7), removing the roes. Lay the scallops in a small dish in a single layer. Pour the cold pickling liquor over them and cover tightly with cling film to keep them submerged. Place in the fridge for 4 hours.

Put all the ingredients for the wine reduction into a pan and bring to the boil, stirring once or twice to encourage the sugar to dissolve, then simmer uncovered until reduced right down to a syrupy dressing. Leave to cool.

Before serving, take the scallops out of the fridge and leave them to come to room temperature for 30 minutes.

To serve, spoon the red wine dressing equally onto each plate. Mix the capers, gherkins and chives with a little wild garlic oil and divide between the plates. Remove the scallops from the pickling liquor, slice them across into discs and arrange on the plates. Finish with a good drizzle of wild garlic oil and crispy fried capers if you like.

Smoking is a traditional ancient method of preservation applied to many foods, but throughout history it has been particularly useful for fish, which goes off relatively quickly. In times past, most fishermen had a smokehouse attached to their cottage. Typically, they would salt the fish for storage, then dry it and smoke it with heat for eating. With refrigeration and freezers, smoking is no longer necessary for preserving, but the technique is still used for the wonderful flavours it lends to the fish.

Over time, the ancient smoking process has been adapted and refined. Nowadays there are basically two types of smoking: cold and hot. Cold smoking takes place between 28 and 32°C, which does not cook the fish or eliminate pathogens, so it is essential to refrigerate the fish. Smoked salmon is the most popular cold-smoked fish. Hot smoking, which is carried out between 70 and 80°C, does cook the fish and changes the texture. The best example of hot-smoked fish is smoked mackerel, which is a particular favourite of mine.

There are now two methods of smoking: traditional and mechanical. For the former, the fish is suspended in smokehouses over smouldering wood, usually overnight, so it slowly takes on the smokiness.

With mechanical smoking, smoke is distilled and used in liquid or solid form, so the process is akin to painting on the flavour. It's a quick, cheap way to produce smoked fish for supermarkets, but it's not great in my opinion.

Traditionally smoked seafood is far superior to its commercial counterpart, so buy this, unless, of course, you are going to smoke the fish yourself, which I would definitely recommend.

Smoking fish is an adventure! You will, of course, need something to smoke it in.

SMOKED

Now that can be an actual smoker, either a Bradley smoker, which I use, or a Big Green Egg or, if you know a good carpenter, he could make you one – like a shed. Or, if you don't want to go to the expense of a purpose-built smoker, you can simply use a large bucket or metal box with some holes drilled into it. You will also need untreated wood shavings. Don't make the mistake of using treated wood, which I did once; it lent a rather peculiar chemical taste!

For hot smoking, you can get really good inexpensive stovetop smokers and I'd recommend buying one of these. You put wood shavings in the bottom of it and get these smoking over a flame, then place your fish on the rack, put it inside the smoker and slide on the lid – it's as simple as that. Make sure you have your extractor on full though – you will need it!

Obviously, the size of the fish or shellfish will determine how long you smoke it for.

You can smoke pretty much any seafood, so experiment, but be prepared for highs and lows, hopefully more highs!

BEST SEAFOOD FOR COLD SMOKING
Salmon, sea trout, bream, trout; also try bass, grey mullet, mackerel, mussels, oysters.

BEST SEAFOOD FOR HOT SMOKING
Salmon, sea trout, trout, bream (all types), bass, grey mullet, mackerel, cod, hake, haddock, whiting, red mullet, horse mackerel.

ACCOMPANIMENTS & GARNISHES
Horseradish yoghurt (page 35), beetroot and apple chutney, tomato water dressing (page 24), smoked tomatoes (page 60), fennel marmalade (page 58), marinated beetroot, treacle bread (page 218).

Smoked gilthead bream
with fennel marmalade

Bream is a lovely fish to smoke – its flesh has a slight oiliness that makes it ideal. Serving it with a veg marmalade may sound unusual but fennel and orange is a great combination that swims so well with the smoky bream. This recipe would work with any of the bream family and I've even done it with a trigger fish!

Serves 4
2 wild gilthead bream, about 600g each, filleted, skinned and pin-boned (see pages 192–4)
Oak chips for smoking

Cure
100g sea salt
100g caster sugar
40g fennel herb
70ml white wine

Fennel marmalade
2 white onions, peeled and sliced
2 garlic cloves, peeled and chopped
100ml white wine vinegar
2 thyme sprigs, leaves only, chopped
2 fennel bulbs, outer layer removed
A little olive oil for cooking
50g caster sugar
Finely grated zest of 1 orange
Sea salt

Bitter orange crème fraîche
200ml full-fat crème fraîche
Finely grated zest of 1 orange, plus 1–2 tbsp juice
2 tsp chopped fennel herb

To finish
Olive oil for dressing
Fennel herb to garnish

For the cure, blitz all the ingredients together in a food processor for 1 minute.

Lay the bream fillets on a tray and pour the cure over them. Make sure the fish is evenly coated all over. Cover with cling film and leave to cure in the fridge for 2 hours.

Set up your smoker for cold smoking. Wash off the cure well with cold water and pat the fish dry with kitchen paper. Lay the fish fillets on the smoking rack and smoke for 30 minutes. Remove the fish from the smoker and place in the fridge to chill for 30 minutes.

For the fennel marmalade, put the onions, garlic, wine vinegar and thyme in a small pan over a medium heat until the liquid has reduced right down, taking care to avoid burning the onions.

Meanwhile, slice the fennel thinly. Heat a large non-stick frying pan over a medium heat. When hot, add a drizzle of olive oil, then the fennel and sugar and cook for 2 minutes. Now add the onion mixture and simmer until the juice has reduced to almost nothing. Add the orange zest and season with salt to taste. Allow to cool, then place in the fridge to chill.

For the orange crème fraîche, put the crème fraîche into a bowl and whisk in the orange zest and enough juice to loosen it slightly. Whisk in the fennel herb and a little salt to taste.

To serve, slice the bream fairly thinly and lay it on 4 plates. Place a heaped spoonful of fennel marmalade on top and serve the orange crème fraîche on the side. Dress the fish with a little olive oil, garnish with fennel and serve.

Smoked trout and tomatoes with horseradish and rocket mayonnaise

I caught my first brown trout fly-fishing on the Test River near Romsey whilst writing this book and this dish is inspired by that day. The flavour of wild trout is incomparable to that of farmed trout, which can taste muddy and a little dull. In order to thrive in tidal and fast-flowing water conditions, river trout develop muscle and their flesh has a fantastic, almost sweet flavour. Brown trout is well suited to smoking, owing to its natural fat content. A smoked tomato salad is an ideal partner.

Serves 4 as a starter or light lunch
4 trout fillets, about 125g each
4 plum tomatoes
1 red onion, peeled and finely sliced
1 Dutch red chilli, deseeded and finely chopped
80g pine nuts, toasted
About 100ml lemon oil (see page 214)
Cornish sea salt and freshly ground black pepper
Oak chips for smoking

Cure
100g sea salt
100g caster sugar
Finely grated zest of 1 lemon
2 garlic cloves, peeled and chopped
1 tbsp chopped rosemary

Horseradish and rocket mayonnaise
2 egg yolks
1½ tsp white wine vinegar
2 tbsp good-quality creamed horseradish
250ml olive oil
70g rocket leaves, chopped

To serve
A handful of rocket leaves

For the cure, mix together the sea salt, sugar, lemon zest, garlic and rosemary. Lay the trout fillets on a tray and pour the cure over them, making sure it is evenly distributed and the fish fillets are covered all over. Cover with cling film and leave to cure in the fridge for 3 hours.

Set up your smoker with the oak chips for hot smoking and heat up to get it smoking. Wash off the cure from the fish with cold water and pat dry with kitchen paper. Lay the fish on the smoking rack and smoke for 15 minutes.

To make the mayonnaise, put the egg yolks, wine vinegar and horseradish into a bowl and whisk to combine. Slowly whisk in the olive oil, drop by drop to begin with, then in a steady stream until it is all incorporated and the mayonnaise is thick. Stir in the chopped rocket leaves and season with salt and pepper to taste. Cover and keep in the fridge until needed.

Thinly slice the tomatoes, removing the core. Lay the tomato slices on a tray that fits in the smoker and scatter the red onion, chilli and pine nuts on top. Drizzle with 2 tbsp lemon oil and season with salt and pepper.

Remove the fish from the smoker, then put the tray of tomatoes into the smoker and smoke for 2 minutes. Meanwhile, carefully flake the fish and dress the rocket leaves in lemon oil.

To serve, remove the tomatoes, chilli, onion and pine nuts from the smoker and arrange on individual plates. Place the smoked trout flakes alongside and dress with more lemon oil. Scatter the rocket leaves over the top and serve with the rocket mayonnaise on the side.

Smoked grey mullet with apple, cider and brown butter dressing

I created this dish for my Academy at Cornwall College when the students had been learning about smoking. Grey mullet does get a bad reputation owing to the estuary fish that hang out around dodgy areas, but don't let that put you off – the fish that are caught out at sea are great. Their oiliness gives them a unique flavour and makes them ideal for smoking. The cider and apples mixed with the smoked butter create a lovely, unusual dressing.

Serves 2

1 grey mullet, about 1.5kg, scaled, filleted and
    pin-boned (see pages 192–4)
Finely grated zest of 1 lime
Light olive oil for marinating and dressing
Cornish sea salt
Oak chips for smoking

Apple, cider and brown butter dressing

200g unsalted butter
1 garlic clove, peeled and crushed
1 rosemary sprig
200ml dry cider
50ml cider vinegar
50g caster sugar
1 banana shallot, peeled and finely chopped
2 green apples, halved, cored and thinly sliced
2 large gherkins, diced
2 tsp capers in brine, rinsed and drained
4 sage leaves, sliced and chopped
1 tbsp finely chopped curly parsley

To serve

2 large handfuls of watercress, picked

Place the fish on a tray and sprinkle with salt and the lime zest. Drizzle with olive oil, cover with cling film and leave to marinate in the fridge for 2 hours.

Set up your smoker with the oak chips for hot smoking and heat up to get it smoking.

To make the dressing, melt the butter in a pan over a medium heat with the garlic and rosemary and heat until the butter turns golden, then remove from the heat.

In another pan, heat the cider and cider vinegar with the sugar and shallot to dissolve the sugar, then bring to a simmer and cook until the liquid becomes syrupy. Remove from the heat. Strain the butter and add it to the reduction.

Place the fish on the smoking rack and smoke for 5–10 minutes until cooked.

Meanwhile, add the apples, gherkins, capers, sage and parsley to the dressing. Taste and add salt if required.

Spoon the dressing over a large platter. Place the cooked fish on top and scatter some of the watercress around. Serve the rest of the watercress on the side.

Hot-smoked mackerel fish cakes with gooseberry jam

Mackerel and gooseberries is a classic pairing and my zingy, punchy gooseberry jam works so well with these little hot smoky fish cakes. Fun to eat, they are perfect party food. If you are entertaining a crowd, treble the recipe and serve the gooseberry jam as a dipping sauce.

Serves 6 as a starter
3 large baking potatoes
Light olive oil for cooking
1 large leek, washed, halved lengthways and
    finely sliced
2 garlic cloves, peeled and finely chopped
4 fillets of hot-smoked mackerel, skinned and
    pin-boned
2 tbsp chopped chervil
75g plain flour for coating
2 eggs, beaten
75g white breadcrumbs
Oil for deep-frying
Cornish sea salt and freshly ground black pepper

Gooseberry jam
Light olive oil for cooking
1 shallot, peeled and chopped
500g gooseberries, topped and tailed
50g unsalted butter
50g caster sugar
50ml white wine
20ml white wine vinegar

To serve
Lime wedges

Heat the oven to 200°C/Gas 6. Put the potatoes on a baking tray, placing each one on a little bed of salt, and bake in the oven for 1 hour.

To make the gooseberry jam, place a large saucepan over a medium heat and add a drizzle of olive oil. When it is hot, add the shallot and sweat for 1 minute without colouring. Add the gooseberries and cook for 2 minutes, then add the butter, sugar, wine and wine vinegar.

Cover and cook for 15 minutes, then remove the lid and continue to cook until the liquid has reduced right down to almost nothing and the mixture is very nearly starting to catch. Season with a pinch of salt.

Tip into a blender and blitz until smooth, then transfer the jam to a bowl and set aside to cool.

To make the fish cakes, cut the baked potatoes in half, scoop out the flesh and press it through a potato ricer into a large bowl – you need 200g cooked potato.

Place a small frying pan over a medium heat and add a drizzle of olive oil. When it is hot, add the leek and garlic and sweat for 2 minutes without colouring, then transfer to a plate to cool slightly.

Flake the smoked mackerel and add to the potato with the chervil. Add the cooled leek and garlic, season with salt and pepper and mix well. Shape the mixture into balls, each about 30g. Roll the balls firmly, then place on a tray and refrigerate for 30 minutes to firm up.

Have the flour, eggs and breadcrumbs ready in 3 separate bowls. Heat the oil in a deep-fryer to 180°C. One at a time, pass the mackerel balls through the flour, then the egg and finally the breadcrumbs. Once coated, place on a tray.

Deep-fry the fish cakes in the hot oil in batches for 2 minutes until golden. Remove and drain on kitchen paper, then season with salt.

Pile the fish cakes onto warm plates and serve with lime wedges and the gooseberry jam. If you have any jam left over, it will keep in the fridge for a couple of weeks – it's delicious with pork and duck as well as mackerel.

Smoked mussel and oyster soup with seaweed and stout toast

Ok, so I am lucky that I live by the sea and have some of the best mussels and oysters growing in the nearby Camel Estuary, but you should be able to get hold of some of these wonderful bivalves with a bit of searching around. Oysters and mussels seem to be at their best in winter and a big bowl of this soup with a chunk of my seaweed and stout bread is just the thing for a cold day.

Serves 4
750g live mussels
12 live oysters
100ml double cream
A little olive oil for cooking
1 white onion, peeled and finely chopped
2 garlic cloves, peeled and finely chopped
1 celery stick, de-stringed and sliced
1 fennel bulb, outer layer removed, diced
100ml white wine
300ml fish stock (see page 213)
1 large potato, peeled and diced
2 tsp chopped tarragon
2 tsp chopped chervil
2 tsp chopped chives
2 tsp chopped flat-leaf parsley
Cornish sea salt and freshly ground black pepper
Oak chips for smoking

To serve
Seaweed and stout bread (see page 219),
   or other good rustic bread

Wash the mussels and pull away the hairy beard attached to one end of the shell. Discard any that are open and refuse to close when sharply tapped, and any with damaged shells. Open the oysters (see page 204) and strain off their juice through a muslin-lined sieve into a bowl.

Set up your smoker with the oak chips for hot smoking and heat up to get it smoking.

Lay the mussels on the wire rack in your smoker with the drip-tray underneath to catch the juices. Smoke the mussels for about 8 minutes until they all open up. Take them out of the smoker and pick out the meat from the shells; discard any that remain closed. Tip the saved juices into a bowl.

Lay the shucked oysters on the rack and smoke for 4 minutes. Put the mussels and oysters together on a plate, cover and chill.

Meanwhile, pour the cream into a heatproof bowl that fits inside the smoker. Place in the smoker, then turn off the heat and leave the cream inside for 20 minutes.

Heat a large saucepan and add a drizzle of olive oil. When it is hot, add the onion, garlic, celery and fennel and sweat for 2 minutes without colouring. Pour in the wine, fish stock and retained mussel and oyster juices, then add the potato. Bring to a simmer and cook for about 15 minutes until the potato is just cooked. Season with salt and pepper to taste.

When you are ready to serve, slice and toast your bread. Add the mussels and smoked cream to the soup and simmer for 1 minute, then add the oysters and chopped herbs and remove from the heat. Taste to check the seasoning.

Ladle the soup equally into 4 warm bowls and serve with the hot toast.

Smoked lobster with saffron and basil mayonnaise

For me, lobsters need to be bought live and cooked and eaten immediately; they never taste the same to me when they are reheated. There are some pretty bold flavours in this dish, but don't worry, meaty lobster can handle it. Just make sure you get everything ready before you dispatch your lobsters.

Serves 4
2 live lobsters, about 800g each
Cornish sea salt and freshly ground black pepper
Oak chips for smoking

Saffron and basil mayonnaise
2 egg yolks
Juice of ½ lemon
½ tsp saffron strands
½ tsp cayenne pepper
150ml light rapeseed oil
3 spring onions, trimmed and finely sliced
6 basil leaves, finely sliced

Saffron oil
2 banana shallots, peeled and finely chopped
2 garlic cloves, peeled and finely chopped
½ tsp saffron strands
200ml cold-pressed rapeseed oil

Dressing
500ml lobster stock (see page 213)
Juice of 1 lemon

Place the live lobsters in the freezer for an hour before cooking to put them to sleep. Put one lobster on a board and firmly insert the tip of a strong, sharp cook's knife into the cross on the head to kill it instantly. Repeat with the other lobster. Now carefully cut the lobsters in half lengthways from head to tail. Remove the stomach sac and the dark intestinal tract that runs along the length of the tail. Put the 4 lobster halves on a tray and set aside.

For the mayonnaise, put the egg yolks, lemon juice, saffron and cayenne in a bowl and whisk to combine. Slowly whisk in the oil, drop by drop to begin with, then in a steady stream until it is all incorporated and the mayonnaise is thick. Season with salt and pepper to taste. Cover and refrigerate until needed.

For the saffron oil, put the chopped shallots and garlic, saffron and rapeseed oil in a small pan and heat to about 80°C, then remove from the heat and set aside.

For the dressing, boil the lobster stock to reduce down to 150ml. Add this to the saffron oil with the lemon juice; set aside.

Set up your smoker with the oak chips for hot smoking and heat up to get it smoking. Place the lobster halves on the rack, trickle a couple of spoonfuls of the saffron dressing over each half and season with salt and pepper. Place in the hot smoker for 10 minutes.

To finish the mayonnaise, stir through the spring onions and basil. Check the seasoning.

Place a lobster half on each warm plate, spoon over some of the dressing and serve at once, with the saffron mayonnaise on the side.

In recent years I've come to appreciate how a fish that has been steamed has the purest flavour of all. If you want to know what a particular fish or shellfish really tastes like then the answer is to steam it. You'll have a wonderful clean flavour and succulent flesh – as long as it has been cooked correctly.

For steaming, it is imperative to use super-fresh fish. Techniques like roasting and pan-frying can hide slightly older fish, as the caramelised flavours produced can mask the pure taste of the fish. Steaming, however, is one technique that will tell you if your fish is old – not only in taste, but also in appearance. If, once steamed, your fish is off-white, even slightly yellow, rather than pearly white, it is not spanking fresh.

Such a gentle heat works like magic, especially with delicately textured fish, like brill and plaice. Steaming is also the healthiest way to cook fish and shellfish, as it locks in the nutrients as well as the flavour – and you can avoid adding any oil or butter if you wish.

You will, of course, need a steamer of some sort to cook your fish. I've found that using a Chinese bamboo steamer works a treat. But then the Chinese have been steaming fish successfully for a very long time so they should know how to do it. They originally used stoneware steamers before inventing the familiar bamboo steamers with their slatted bases. They use them for everything, not just fish.

STEAMED

Alternatively, you can use a metal steamer that fits over a saucepan – you'll need about 5–7cm boiling water in the pan. Either way, make sure the steamer basket is not touching the water and cover with a tight-fitting lid to seal in the steam.

You can steam small to medium whole fish, such as bream or bass, but I usually steam fillets as they cook more evenly. Often I'll wrap these in baking parchment to protect them, or in wild garlic or spinach leaves to lend flavour too. The cooking time depends on the size and thickness of the fish. As a rough guide, a medium-thick 200g piece of fish takes about 8 minutes.

Steaming is also the technique used to open bivalves – mainly mussels, cockles and clams. Typically, a little wine or cider is heated in a large pan, then the shellfish are added and the lid fitted tightly. The shells open up in the steam created by the liquor in minutes – ready to be picked or eaten straight from the shell.

BEST SEAFOOD FOR STEAMING
Plaice, lemon sole, brill, turbot, bass, bream, salmon, mussels, cockles, clams.

BEST ACCOMPANIMENTS
Braised fennel with a lime dressing, lemon sauce (page 72), watercress sauce (page 76), mushroom ketchup (page 215), saffron and roasted garlic potato purée (page 159).

Lemon sole steamed
in wild garlic leaves
with lemon sauce

Ultra-fresh lemon sole is amazing steamed, as the gentle, moist heat complements the delicate flesh of the fish perfectly. Wild garlic is shooting out of the ground when the best lemon sole is available to me, during April and May, and it works so well with the zingy, rich lemon and parsley butter sauce.

Serves 4
2 lemon sole, about 600g each, filleted and skinned
    (see pages 185–6)
16 large wild garlic leaves
Cornish sea salt and freshly ground black pepper

Lemon sauce
2 shallots, peeled and finely chopped
1 garlic clove, peeled and finely chopped
2 lemon thyme sprigs
100ml white wine
50ml double cream
250g unsalted butter, in pieces
2 tbsp chopped flat-leaf parsley

To serve
Basil oil (see page 214) to finish
Lemon wedges

Heat up your steamer (or steamer basket over a pan of simmering water). Check over the fish fillets for any little bits of skin or small bones, then sort into 2 fillets per portion, making the portions roughly the same size. Season with salt and pepper. Put the garlic leaves in the steamer for just a few seconds to wilt them, then lift out. (This will make it easier to wrap the fish.)

Lay 4 garlic leaves out on a surface, overlapping the edges to make a sheet. Place a fish portion in the middle and wrap the leaves around the fish. Repeat with the remaining garlic leaves and fish portions to make 4 parcels. Set aside.

To make the lemon sauce, put the shallots, garlic, lemon thyme and wine in a small pan over a medium heat and let bubble until the wine has reduced down to almost nothing. Add the cream and lower the heat.

Now add the butter, piece by piece, whisking continuously. Do not allow to boil, but retain a warm heat. When all the butter is incorporated, remove the thyme. Season the sauce with salt and pepper to taste, and add the chopped parsley. Keep warm until ready to serve.

Place the lemon sole parcels in the steamer, put the lid on and steam for 6 minutes, until the fish is cooked but slightly rare in the middle. Remove the steamer from the pan.

Spoon the lemon sauce onto warm plates and place the fish parcels on top. Finish with a drizzle of basil oil and add a lemon wedge to each plate.

I would serve this with something fresh and crunchy, like a baby gem salad lightly dressed with lemon and olive oil.

Steamed bass and tomatoes with sardine and tomato ketchup

Bass really benefits from steaming, though it's rarely cooked this way. I love the idea of creating sauces and dressings from the cooking process. Here the juices from the tomatoes and fish produce a wonderful, tasty dressing as they steam together with a little olive oil. And I've added tinned sardines to my ketchup recipe – to raise the ever-popular tomato ketchup to new fishy heights!

Serves 2
2 bass fillets, about 200g each, pin-boned
2 ripe plum tomatoes
1 garlic clove, peeled and chopped
1 rosemary sprig, leaves only, chopped
A little olive oil
A little caster sugar
Cornish sea salt and freshly ground black pepper

Sardine and tomato ketchup
A little olive oil
2 red onions, peeled and chopped
2 garlic cloves, peeled and chopped
1kg ripe tomatoes, chopped
75g caster sugar
2 bay leaves
1 rosemary sprig, leaves only, chopped
200ml red wine vinegar
2 x 120g tins good-quality sardines in tomato sauce

To serve
A large handful of rocket leaves

First make the ketchup. Heat a large pan over a medium heat and add a drizzle of olive oil. When hot, add the onions and garlic and cook for 2 minutes until the onions start to turn translucent. Add the tomatoes, sugar, bay leaves and chopped rosemary to the pan and cook for 15 minutes until the tomatoes have broken down. Continue to cook until the tomato liquid has reduced right down, almost to nothing.

Now add the wine vinegar and sardines and boil for 5 minutes. Remove the bay leaves.

Transfer the contents of the pan to a blender or food processor and blend until smooth, then pass though a sieve into a bowl. Taste for seasoning, adding salt and pepper as required. Transfer the ketchup to a clean container and allow to cool. (This ketchup will keep in the fridge for up to 3 days or you can freeze it for up to a month.)

Heat up your steamer (or steamer basket over a pan of simmering water). Take 2 pieces of baking parchment and fold and scrunch up the sides slightly.

Bring a large pan of salted water to a simmer over a medium heat. Plunge the plum tomatoes into the water for 20 seconds, then transfer to a bowl of iced water. Lift them out and peel away the skins.

Halve the tomatoes lengthways and sprinkle over the garlic, rosemary and olive oil, then season with salt, pepper and sugar. Place the tomatoes on the parchment in the steamer and steam for 5 minutes.

Season the bass fillets, oil them all over and then lay, skin side up, on the parchment in the steamer with the tomatoes. Steam for 6 minutes until cooked.

Lift the fish and tomatoes on the parchment from the steamer. Using a spatula, carefully transfer them to warm plates. Drizzle over all the cooking juices from the parchment and serve, with peppery rocket leaves and the ketchup on the side.

Salmon with watercress sauce and smoked onions

This dish is great for entertaining because it's all done in advance and everyone – or almost everyone – loves salmon. The smoky flavours are in the onions and dressing rather than the fish, which is a nice surprise when you eat it. If you don't have a smoker, a steamer works well.

Serves 4
4 portions of organic farmed or wild salmon fillet, about 200g each, skinned
3 white onions (the size of a tennis ball), peeled
Light rapeseed oil to drizzle
Cornish sea salt and freshly ground black pepper
Oak chips for smoking

Watercress sauce
100ml light rapeseed oil
2 shallots, peeled and finely chopped
2 garlic cloves, peeled and finely chopped
Finely grated zest and juice of 1 lime
6 anchovies in oil, drained and chopped
2 tbsp capers in wine vinegar, drained
300g watercress, picked
2 tbsp wholegrain mustard

To serve
Lime wedges

Heat up your steamer (or a steamer basket large enough to hold the salmon over a pan of simmering water). Meanwhile, cut the onions into wedges and separate into petals. Place them in the steamer and steam for 20 minutes until cooked through but not falling apart. Remove from the steamer. Season the salmon all over and oil it well.

Set up your smoker with the oak chips for hot smoking and heat up to get it smoking. Pour the 100ml rapeseed oil for the sauce into a metal bowl. Add the steamed onions and bowl of oil to the smoker, keeping them separate. Smoke the onions and oil for 30 minutes.

Meanwhile, for the sauce, put the shallots, garlic, lime zest and juice, anchovies, capers and watercress onto a board and chop finely. Transfer to a bowl, add the mustard, mix well and season with salt and pepper to taste. Set aside until the oil is ready.

Carefully place the salmon in the steamer and steam for 8 minutes or until cooked the way you like it. I like mine pink! Remove the oil and onions from the smoker. Let the oil cool slightly and then stir it into the watercress mixture and check the seasoning.

When the fish is done, carefully transfer to warm plates and serve immediately with the watercress sauce, smoked onions and lime wedges on the side. This dish can also be served cold if you prefer.

Mackerel and pollack dumplings in leek and saffron soup

I love Chinese-style steamed dumplings, so I decided to create my own version from fish trimmings one day. Using a combination of oily and white fish gives the dumplings a lovely balance of texture and moisture, and a great flavour. They add another dimension to this delicious leek and saffron soup.

<u>Serves 4</u>

<u>Mackerel and pollack dumplings</u>
300g mackerel fillet, skinned
300g pollack fillet, skinned
A drizzle of light rapeseed oil, plus extra for oiling
2 shallots, peeled and finely chopped
2 garlic cloves, peeled and finely chopped
2 Dutch red chillies, deseeded and finely chopped
1 egg, lightly beaten
 2 tbsp finely chopped flat-leaf parsley
1 tbsp chopped dill
Cornish sea salt and freshly ground black pepper

<u>Leek and saffron soup</u>
A drizzle of cold-pressed rapeseed oil
1 white onion, peeled and chopped
1 garlic clove, peeled and finely chopped
3 leeks, washed and sliced
100g potato, peeled and diced
½ tsp saffron strands
1 litre fish stock (see page 213)
150ml double cream
A drizzle of good olive oil to finish

To make the dumplings, check over the fish fillets for pin bones. Heat a frying pan over a medium heat and add a drizzle of oil, followed by the shallots, garlic and chillies. Sweat for 2 minutes to soften without colouring, then tip out onto a tray to cool.

Put the mackerel and pollack fillet in a food processor and blitz for 30 seconds. Scrape down the sides of the food processor and season the mixture with salt and pepper, then blend for another 30 seconds.

Transfer the mixture to a cold bowl and add the cooled shallot mixture, beaten egg and herbs. Mix well with your hands, then shape into balls, the size of golf balls, and place on a tray. Chill while you make the soup.

To make the soup, heat a saucepan over a medium heat, then add a little oil. When it is hot, add the onion, garlic and leeks and sweat for 3 minutes to soften without colour.

Add the potato and saffron, then pour in the fish stock and season with salt and pepper. Bring to a simmer and simmer gently until the potato is cooked. Add the cream, bring back to a simmer and cook for another minute. Taste and adjust the seasoning as necessary. Transfer to a blender and blend until just smooth. Return to the clean pan.

Heat up your steamer (or steamer basket over a pan of simmering water). Take the dumplings from the fridge, oil them all over and season with a little salt. Line your steamer with silicone paper. Place the dumplings in the steamer, cover and cook for 5 minutes. Gently reheat the soup.

Ladle the soup equally into 4 warm bowls and share the dumplings between them. Add a drizzle of olive oil and serve at once.

Mussels in beer with onion, garlic and parsley

When I opened my first restaurant at the St Enodoc Hotel, I was sitting on our beautiful terrace looking out across Porthilly to the Rock Shellfish mussel and oyster farm whilst downing a pint of Doom Bar from Sharp's Brewery just up the road. There and then, this simple dish of mussels and beer was created. Sometimes the inspiration for a dish is right in front of you... Magic!

<u>Serves 2</u>
1kg live mussels
A drizzle of rapeseed or olive oil
50g butter
1 white onion, peeled and finely chopped
1 garlic clove, peeled and finely chopped
200ml beer (Doom Bar or other good-quality bitter)
3 tbsp chopped curly parsley

Wash the mussels and pull away the hairy beard attached to one end of the shell. Discard any that are open and refuse to close when sharply tapped, as they will be dead, and any with damaged shells.

Place a large saucepan (one with a tight-fitting lid) over a high heat. When hot, add a drizzle of oil and the butter, quickly followed by the onion and garlic. Cook for 30 seconds, then add the mussels. Count to 10 and then pour in the beer and cover with the lid. Cook for 2 minutes.

Remove the lid to check if the mussels are open. If they are not, put the lid back on and continue to cook, checking every 30 seconds until all, or most of them, are open.

When the mussels are cooked, add the chopped parsley, toss to mix and divide between warm bowls or tip into a large bowl to share. Serve with chips or bread... and more beer.

Clam, seaweed and broad bean broth

This dish has its roots in Japanese cookery, but the seaweeds are relatively easy to find in the UK. If you can't get hold of them you can make the broth with instant dashi stock, which is available from most supermarkets. You could use mussels or other shellfish in place of clams, or even a mixture.

Serves 4
2kg live palourde and/or razor clams
2 shallots, peeled and chopped
400ml dry cider
800ml fish stock (see page 213)
4cm piece of dried kombu seaweed, soaked for
    30 minutes
160g freshly podded broad beans
3 tbsp pickled dulse seaweed
Juice of 1 lime
Cornish sea salt and freshly ground black pepper

To finish
8 basil leaves, sliced in half
Cold-pressed rapeseed oil to drizzle

Wash the clams and discard any that are open and refuse to close when sharply tapped, as they will be dead, and any with damaged shells.

To make the broth, place a large pan (that will hold all the clams and has a well-fitting lid) over a medium heat. When it is hot, add the clams, shallots and cider and put the lid on. Steam for

2–3 minutes until the clams open up. Tip the contents of the pan into a colander set over a bowl, to collect all that lovely clam juice.

Heat the fish stock and add the clam juice and kombu seaweed. Take off the heat and let the seaweed infuse its magic and clam juice settle for 30 minutes (any fragments of shell and sand will sink to the bottom). In the meantime, pick out the meat from the clam shells (see page 205 for razor clam preparation); set aside.

Now carefully pour off the clam juice and stock mixture into another pan, leaving the sediment and seaweed behind.

Bring a pan of salted water to the boil, add the broad beans and cook for 2 minutes, then drain and plunge into iced water. Drain and slip the beans out of their skins, unless they are young and the skins are tender.

Bring the clam juice and fish stock mixture to the boil. Taste and season with salt if you think it needs it and a little pepper. Add the clams, broad beans, pickled dulse and lime juice and heat through gently.

Share the broth between warm bowls, scatter over the basil and drizzle with a little rapeseed oil to serve.

Poached fish has never really been fashionable, perhaps because it was once associated with convalescent food and typically served as a bland and flavourless dish. Yet poaching can be one of the most flexible and adventurous of cooking techniques for fish and shellfish.

For a start, you can poach seafood in a variety of different liquids, from a classic court bouillon, fish or shellfish stock to salted butter, various oils, milk or cream. I have used a different poaching liquid for each of the dishes in this chapter, to show you the flexibility.

So why am I so keen on the poaching technique? Well, there are a number of reasons. Poaching is like cooking and marinating at the same time. Generally, the seafood will take on board the flavours of what you are poaching it in, to delicious effect. You just need to make sure that those flavours are not so intense that they overpower the natural taste of the seafood. Another advantage is that as poaching is a gentle method, it preserves the nutrients in the fish well.

Poaching is also a technique that gives you a little leeway when you are cooking. Fish can overcook and become dry quickly under a grill or in a hot, dry frying pan, but poaching is a little more forgiving because the seafood is immersed in liquid.

You can poach seafood either on the hob or in the oven. Poaching on the hob calls for a nice deep, large pan that can hold the liquid and the fish or shellfish comfortably.

POACHED

The heat that you poach at is slightly under a simmer, i.e. 90–95°C. At this temperature, the liquor should not be bubbling but you should see steam rising from the surface.

For oven poaching, preheat the oven to about 160°C/Gas 3 and put the fish into a suitable oven dish. Warm the poaching liquor in a pan until hot but not scalding, then pour it over the fish to two-thirds cover it. Put the lid on or cover the dish with greaseproof paper and foil. At this temperature, you will get perfectly cooked succulent fish and a lovely tasty stock to use as a base for a sauce or dressing.

More often than not I use either a salted butter or a highly flavoured court bouillon for poaching. Both of these bring something special to the fish.

BEST SEAFOOD FOR POACHING
Scallops, large bass, large brill, salmon, large cod, large hake, large ling, lobster, monkfish, mussels, oysters, large plaice, sea trout, large turbot.

ACCOMPANIMENTS & GARNISHES
Pickled mushroom dressing, (page 90), cucumber chutney (page 146), pickled carrots (page 174), tomatoes poached in olive oil (page 93).

Salmon poached in tarragon vinegar with carrots in brown butter

Poaching fish in vinegar isn't new – a classic French court bouillon includes vinegar – but it isn't as popular as it once was. It takes skill to poach a lovely, thick piece of fish, and salmon is a good one to try first. Its slightly oily flesh is forgiving and will stay moist if you slightly overdo it. The tarragon vinegar cuts the richness of the salmon and butter perfectly.

Serves 4
4 portions of salmon fillet, about 200g each, pin-boned
2 carrots, peeled
200ml white wine
200ml white wine vinegar
400ml water
50g caster sugar
10 tarragon sprigs
Sea salt

Carrots in brown butter
250g salted butter
8 small carrots, peeled and halved lengthways, or 24 baby carrots
1 garlic clove, peeled and finely chopped
2 tsp chopped tarragon

Cut the carrots lengthways into fine ribbons, using a vegetable peeler or mandoline. Pour the wine, wine vinegar and water into a saucepan and add the sugar, a pinch of salt, the carrot ribbons and tarragon sprigs. Bring to the boil, lower the heat and simmer for 2 minutes. Take off the heat and leave to infuse for 30 minutes.

Meanwhile, for the brown butter, heat the butter in a pan over a medium-low heat until melted and starting to bubble. At this stage, lower the heat and continue to cook until the butter turns brown and has a nutty aroma; don't let it burn. Immediately remove from the heat and strain through a muslin-lined sieve into a bowl.

Add the halved or whole baby carrots to a pan containing enough cold water to just cover them and add some salt. Bring to the boil, lower the heat and simmer for about 10 minutes until the carrots are almost cooked. Drain and return them to the pan. Add 50ml of the brown butter with the chopped garlic and warm through over a low heat. Season with salt to taste and remove from the heat.

Drain the carrot ribbons, reserving the liquor; set aside.

To cook the salmon, bring the reserved liquor to a simmer in a fairly wide pan and add the fish fillets, making sure they are fully submerged. Remove the pan from the heat, cover and leave to stand for 10 minutes; the fish will cook in the residual heat. To check the fish is done, carefully lift out a portion and insert a small knife into the thickest point, hold it there for 5 seconds and then place it against the back of your wrist; it should feel warm, not cold or hot.

Once the fish is ready, for the dressing, combine 75ml of the poaching liquor with 150ml brown butter, warm through and add the chopped tarragon. Place a portion of salmon on each warm plate. Divide the carrot ribbons and brown butter carrots between the plates and spoon the dressing over the fish and carrots to serve.

Plaice poached in butter with leeks, and parsley and mustard mash

Poached on the bone, plaice is great. Poached in butter, it's even better! This is a fish that is prone to drying, but the butter keeps the flesh deliciously moist. Lemon sole and brill similarly benefit from being cooked this way.

Serves 4
2 plaice, about 1kg each, fins trimmed, head
    removed and split down the centre bone
500g salted butter
2 bay leaves
3 garlic cloves, peeled and crushed
1 large thyme sprig
8 small leeks, outer leaves removed and cut
    across in half, or 12 baby leeks, trimmed
Cornish sea salt and freshly ground black pepper

Parsley and mustard mash
3 large baking potatoes
150ml whole milk
4 tbsp chopped flat-leaf parsley
1–2 tbsp English mustard, to taste

To serve
Lemon wedges

Heat your oven to 220°C/Gas 7. For the mash, put the potatoes on an oven tray and bake for 1 hour or until tender.

Put the butter, bay leaves, garlic and thyme in a pan and warm over a low heat until the butter has melted. Add the leeks and cook until the butter starts to turn golden, then remove from the heat and leave to cool.

Once cooled, strain off most of the butter into a roasting tin large enough to hold the plaice. Transfer the leeks to a tray, ready to warm through to serve. Reserve the rest of the butter.

When the potatoes are cooked, set aside until cool enough to handle. Lower the oven setting to 180°C/Gas 4.

For the mash, bring the milk to a simmer in a pan and remove from the heat. Cut the potatoes in half, scoop out the flesh and pass through a potato ricer into a bowl, or mash with a potato masher. Fold in the milk and then add enough of the reserved poaching butter to give a soft mash. Add the chopped parsley and mustard and season with salt and pepper to taste.

To cook the fish, bring the butter in the roasting tin to a simmer. Carefully add the fish and cook in the oven for about 12 minutes. Meanwhile, warm the mash and leeks.

To check the fish is done, carefully lift a piece out of the butter and insert a small knife at the thickest point, hold it there for 5 seconds and then place it against the back of your wrist; it should feel warm, not cold or hot.

Scoop the mash onto warm plates and add the leeks. Carefully lift the plaice onto the plates, spoon over some of the butter and season with a little salt. Serve at once, with lemon wedges.

Monkfish wrapped in pancetta with pickled mushroom dressing

Monkfish has a lovely meaty texture and wrapping it in pancetta really enhances the flavour. I poach the fish first, to keep it moist, then pan-fry it to colour the bacon and give it that great roasted flavour. Pickled mushrooms for acidity, together with the sharp, sweet freshness from the grapes, work brilliantly with the salty bacon and succulent fish.

Serves 4
4 filleted portions of monkfish, about 200g each, trimmed (see page 199)
12 thin slices of smoked pancetta
1–2 tbsp light rapeseed oil

Pickled mushroom dressing
100ml oaked Chardonnay or similar white wine
50ml white wine vinegar
50g caster sugar
2 garlic cloves, peeled and finely chopped
2 tbsp light rapeseed oil
200g chestnut mushrooms, quartered
100g shimeji mushrooms, left whole
2 shallots, peeled and chopped
2 tbsp sherry vinegar
100ml cold-pressed rapeseed oil
2 tsp chopped flat-leaf parsley
20 grapes, deseeded and quartered
Cornish sea salt and freshly ground black pepper

Wrap each monkfish portion in 3 pancetta slices, overlapping them slightly to enclose the fish, then overwrap in all-purpose cling film and tie the ends to ensure the parcels are watertight. Place in the fridge until ready to cook.

To make the dressing, put the wine, wine vinegar and sugar in a pan over a medium heat to dissolve the sugar, then let bubble to reduce by half. Add half of the garlic and set aside.

Heat a frying pan over a medium heat and add the 2 tbsp oil. When hot, add all the mushrooms and cook for 1 minute, then add the shallots and remaining garlic and cook for another minute. Pour in half the wine reduction, add the sherry vinegar and take off the heat. Set aside.

Bring a wide, shallow pan of water to a simmer and add the wrapped monkfish parcels. When the water returns to a simmer, turn the heat right down and cook gently for 10 minutes. Lift the parcels out of the water and leave to rest, still wrapped in the cling film, for 4 minutes.

Meanwhile heat a non-stick frying pan and add a good drizzle of oil. Remove the monkfish parcels from the cling film, saving all the juices; add these juices to the mushrooms. Pat the monkfish parcels dry with kitchen paper and place them in the hot pan. Cook for 2 minutes, turning the parcels so that they colour all over.

Add the remaining wine reduction, rapeseed oil, parsley and grapes to the mushrooms and heat through. Taste for seasoning.

Share the mushroom dressing between warm bowls. Halve the monkfish parcels and arrange on top of the mushrooms. Serve at once.

Tuna poached in oil with tomatoes, garlic and beans

Tuna is landed in Cornwall, but it's a rare occurrence, so I generally use imported albacore, yellowfin or bonito, making sure that they are from sustainable sources. The Italians and Spanish can tuna with amazing olive oil and make fantastic salads with it. I've basically stolen the idea and made it mine by using local rapeseed oil with garlic, beans and tomatoes. If you can't get hold of sustainable fresh tuna, use salmon or sea trout instead.

Serves 4
4 tuna steaks, about 200g each
400ml cold-pressed rapeseed oil
12 garlic cloves (unpeeled)
2 rosemary sprigs
2 bay leaves
20 cherry tomatoes
200g fresh green beans, topped and tailed
400g tin cannellini beans, drained and rinsed
   (or use cooked fresh beans, if you can find them)
Handful of small basil leaves
Finely grated zest and juice of 1 lemon
Cornish sea salt and freshly ground black pepper

To prepare the poaching oil, heat the oven to its lowest setting (about 90°C/Gas ¼). Pour the rapeseed oil into an ovenproof dish (that will hold the tuna steaks in a single layer later) and add the garlic cloves, rosemary and bay leaves. Place in the oven for about 15 minutes to infuse.

Add the cherry tomatoes to the dish and return to the oven for about 40 minutes until they are cooked. Remove them with a slotted spoon, keeping the oil and aromatics in the dish to cook the tuna. Turn the oven up to 160°C/Gas 3.

Bring a pan of water to the boil, add salt, then add the green beans and blanch for 2 minutes until tender but retaining a bite. Drain the beans and plunge into a bowl of ice-cold water to retain their colour.

To cook the tuna, season with salt and pepper, then place the steaks in the dish in the oven, making sure they are completely submerged in the oil. Cook for 10 minutes and then remove from the oven. Transfer the tuna to a warm plate; keep warm.

Add the green and white beans to the oil with the tomatoes and warm through in the oven for 3 minutes. Drain the beans, garlic, tomatoes and herbs in a sieve over a bowl, to save the oil.

Divide the warm tomatoes, beans and garlic between warm plates and place a tuna steak on each plate. Scatter the basil and lemon zest on top. Mix the lemon juice with three times its volume of poaching oil to make a dressing and season with salt and pepper. Trickle the dressing over the tuna and serve.

Brill with mussels, cockles, clams, asparagus and spring onions

Big fillets of brill are brilliant for poaching. When pan-fried or grilled, they can become a bit dry but poaching gives you more control. Cooking them in a shellfish stock with clams, cockles and mussels works particularly well. Fresh asparagus gives this dish a real sense of spring. You might like to throw in a few early season peas and broad beans too – and vary the herbs.

Serves 4

4 brill fillets, about 200g each, skinned and trimmed
12 live mussels, cleaned and beards removed
12 live cockles, cleaned
12 live clams, cleaned
500ml shellfish stock (see page 213)
12 asparagus spears
8 tbsp cold-pressed extra virgin rapeseed oil
3 tbsp white wine vinegar
4 spring onions, trimmed and finely shredded
2 tsp chopped chervil
50g unsalted butter, in pieces
Cornish sea salt and freshly ground black pepper

To open the molluscs, place a large saucepan (that has a tight-fitting lid) over a medium heat. When it is hot, add the mussels, cockles, clams and 100ml shellfish stock and put the lid on. Steam for 2 minutes until the shells open; discard any that remain closed.

Tip the contents of the pan into a colander set over a bowl to catch the cooking liquor. Strain the saved liquor through a muslin-lined sieve into a bowl to get rid of any sand. Clean the pan, ready to cook the fish.

Trim the asparagus and peel the lower end of the stems; set aside ready to cook.

To make the dressing, in a small pan, mix 180ml shellfish stock with the extra virgin oil and wine vinegar. Add the spring onions and chervil and season with salt and pepper.

To cook the brill fillets, pour the remaining shellfish stock, including the strained stock from the molluscs, into the saucepan and bring to a simmer. Season the brill fillets, add them to the stock and cook for 4 minutes. Add the asparagus and molluscs, put the lid on the pan and cook for 2 minutes.

Carefully transfer the brill, molluscs and asparagus to a warmed dish; cover and keep warm. For the sauce, bring the stock to the boil over a high heat and whisk in the butter.

Share the asparagus between 4 warm plates. Place the brill fillets on top and arrange the molluscs around the fish. Spoon over the dressing. Serve with the sauce.

Scallops poached in coconut milk with mangetout, bean sprout and peanut salad

Scallops may be delicate but they can handle punchy flavours, like the Asian ones I've used here. Coconut milk is a perfect medium for poaching fish and shellfish – and an excellent way to infuse fish with other flavours too. The peanut salad brings a lovely texture and zingy heat to the dish.

Serves 4

16 live scallops in the shell
50ml sunflower oil
1 small red onion, peeled and finely sliced
2 garlic cloves, peeled and sliced
1 green chilli, sliced, seeds retained
50g root ginger, peeled and sliced
2 x 400ml tins coconut milk
2 tbsp roughly torn coriander
Cornish sea salt

Mangetout, bean sprout and peanut salad

100g mangetout, finely sliced
Handful of bean sprouts
1 small red onion, peeled and finely sliced
1 green chilli, deseeded and finely sliced
5 tbsp roasted peanuts
2 tbsp roughly torn coriander leaves
Finely grated zest and juice of 1 lime
Generous drizzle of olive oil

Shell and clean the scallops (see pages 206–7).

Heat a wide, medium saucepan over a medium heat and add a drizzle of oil. When the oil is hot, add the onion, garlic, chilli and ginger and cook for 5 minutes until the onion is softened. Pour in the coconut milk, add a pinch of salt, stir and simmer for 5 minutes.

Meanwhile, for the salad, put the mangetout, bean sprouts and red onion into a bowl with the chilli, peanuts and coriander. Toss to mix, season with salt and add the lime zest. Dress with the lime juice and olive oil.

Add the scallops to the coconut milk and poach gently for about 5 minutes. Now add the chopped coriander and take off the heat.

Using a slotted spoon, remove the scallops from the pan and divide them between warm bowls. Add a few ladlefuls of the poaching liquid and arrange some of the salad alongside the scallops. Serve at once, with the rest of the salad in a bowl on the side.

Boiling and braising both involve cooking in liquid. Boiling entails immersing the seafood in a pan of fast-boiling water and is only used to cook crustaceans, such as lobster, crab and scampi; to boil a piece of fish in liquid would be to ruin it.

Braising is a more gentle method of cooking, by totally or partially immersing the fish in liquid. Braising can be done in the oven or on the hob in a covered dish.

Boiling is pretty straightforward. The water needs to be bubbling away rapidly before you add the shellfish and you need to add plenty of salt (around 30g salt per litre of water). If there is not enough salt in the water, the crustacean(s) will become waterlogged and flavour will leach out into the water and be lost. And, of course, you need to time the cooking carefully. The great thing about this technique is that it is consistent – once you've boiled a crab or a lobster correctly you've cracked it.

Braising is an excellent technique for cooking octopus, cuttlefish and big squid. Immersed in their braising liquor, these cephalopods tenderise as they cook slowly and gently for around an hour.

Chunky fish steaks also respond well to braising, but they cook much more quickly. Braised with a few shallots softened in butter and a glug of wine in a suitable pan covered with a tight-fitting lid, a thick piece of fish will emerge beautifully succulent and flavoursome. What's more, you have the added advantage of a lovely braising liquor to use as the base of a sauce. Just add a splash of cream and some freshly chopped herbs or some olive oil and fresh tomato and you have a lovely sauce to accompany your fish. With your prepared ingredients,

BOILED & BRAISED

that should take you all of about 8 minutes to cook. That's convenience food for you!

What I like about braising fish is that it enables me to flavour the fish in any way I like. For example, beer is used to braise the turbot on page 110, but you could use cider, wine or fish stock if you prefer. And the choice of aromatics you can add is endless: herbs, shallot, garlic, a little chilli or ginger perhaps; the choice is yours.

As for boiling, you really cannot beat a freshly boiled crab served with a homemade mayonnaise and some good bread. Just remember the salty cooking water!

I really love the idea of a 'fish boil' – a culinary tradition centred around the Great Lakes in the USA. Friends and family gather to prepare and cook loads of fish and seafood together in a big pot of salty water over an open fire. It sounds great!

BEST SEAFOOD FOR BRAISING
Thick bass, thick brill, big cod, cuttlefish, thick grey mullet, thick hake, thick ling, lobster, monkfish, octopus, big squid, big turbot.

BEST SEAFOOD FOR BOILING
Brown, spider and velvet crabs; lobster, crawfish, prawns, scampi; squat lobsters (if you're lucky enough to find them).

ACCOMPANIMENTS & GARNISHES
Cider vinegar dressing, celeriac and apple salad (page 102), pickled chicory salad (page 108), pickled fennel with orange, saffron potatoes.

Lobster soup,
lobster dumplings

This fantastic dish is ideal for a special meal. It uses the whole lobster, including the shells.

Serves 4
2 live lobsters, about 700–800g each
A little light rapeseed oil for cooking
1 banana shallot, peeled and chopped
1 carrot, peeled and chopped
2 red peppers, deseeded and chopped
1 fennel bulb, trimmed and chopped
4 garlic cloves, peeled and crushed
2 tbsp good-quality tomato purée
1 tsp saffron strands
6 plum tomatoes, chopped
200ml white wine
1 litre fish stock (see page 213)
Cornish sea salt and freshly ground black pepper

Dumplings
200g cod fillet, diced and pin-boned
1 egg
150ml double cream
2 tbsp sliced basil leaves

Red pepper and saffron dressing
1 red pepper, peeled, deseeded and finely sliced
1 garlic clove, peeled and finely diced
1 tbsp white wine shallots (see page 216)
½ tsp saffron strands
80ml extra virgin olive oil

Put the lobsters in the freezer for an hour before cooking. Bring a large pan of water to the boil; salt well. To kill the lobsters, firmly insert the tip of a sturdy knife through the cross on the head. Remove the head; save for the soup. Pull off the claws and pull on the central tail fin to remove the intestinal tract. Add the lobster claws to the boiling water and cook for 2 minutes, then add the tails and cook for a further 2 minutes. Remove and leave until cool enough to handle.

Crack the claws and knuckles and extract the meat. Pull open each tail and remove the meat in one piece; reserve the shells. Put the tails to one side. Chop the claw and knuckle meat together. Heat your oven to 200°C/Gas 6.

For the dumplings, blend the cod, egg and a pinch of salt in a food processor for 1 minute. Scrape down the sides of the bowl and blend for a further 30 seconds, then repeat. With the motor running, slowly add the cream, stopping the machine as soon as it is all incorporated. Transfer to a bowl and fold in the basil and chopped claw meat. Season, cover and chill.

Put the lobster heads and shells in a roasting tray, drizzle with oil and roast in the oven for 45 minutes. Meanwhile, heat a large pan over a medium heat and add a drizzle of oil. Add the shallot, carrot, red peppers, fennel and garlic and cook for 5 minutes, stirring often. Add the tomato purée and cook for another 5 minutes, then add the saffron and tomatoes and cook for a further 5 minutes. Take the pan off the heat.

Smash the roasted shells up in their tray. Place on a medium heat, add the wine and let bubble for 2–3 minutes, stirring to deglaze. Transfer to the soup pan, then pour in the fish stock to cover (if necessary, add a little water). Bring to a simmer, skim, then simmer for 30 minutes. Work the soup through a mouli or large potato ricer. Taste for seasoning and put to one side.

For the dressing, heat a frying pan with a little oil. Add the red pepper and cook for 3 minutes, then add the garlic and cook for another minute. Take off the heat. Add the white wine shallots, saffron and oil, season with salt and set aside.

Shape the chilled dumpling mixture into small balls, the size of golf balls. Heat a little oil in a non-stick frying pan and colour the dumplings.

Reheat the soup in the pan, add the dumplings and simmer for 3 minutes. Meanwhile, slice the lobster tails. Share the dumplings between 4 warm bowls, then pour on the soup. Divide the lobster tail meat between the bowls and drizzle each with a couple of spoonfuls of dressing.

Crab with celeriac and apple salad

Crab meat is superb in the autumn, when apples and celeriac are also at their best. This is a lovely simple dish, with a complex blend of flavours. Try to get hold of live crab – it really does make all the difference and it's fun to prepare!

Serves 4
2 live brown crabs, about 1kg each
Celeriac and apple salad
1 small celeriac
4 celery sticks
1 Granny Smith apple, peeled and grated
2 tsp chopped chives
3 tbsp mustard mayonnaise (see page 213)
Cornish sea salt and freshly ground black pepper
Shallot and apple dressing
2 tsp white wine shallots (see page 216)
1 Granny Smith apple, peeled and cut into 1cm dice
1 tsp chopped chives
2 tbsp lemon juice
100ml cold-pressed rapeseed oil
To finish
Small handful of watercress

Place the crabs in the freezer for an hour before cooking. To cook them, bring a large pan of water to the boil and season it with a lot of salt (make it very salty). Plunge the crabs into the boiling water and cook for 15 minutes. As soon as the crabs are cooked, lift them out onto a tray and leave until cool enough to handle.

Prepare the crabs (as described and shown on pages 202–3), extracting all the white meat from the body, claws and legs, and the brown meat from the top shell. Don't forget to discard the dead man's fingers, stomach sac and hard membranes from the body.

When you have extracted all the crab meat, go through it carefully a couple of times with your fingers to check for fragments of shell and cartilage. You can refrigerate your crab meat or freeze it at this point, but I prefer to eat it straight away.

To prepare the salad, peel and slice the celeriac, then cut into thin strips, the size of matchsticks. De-string the celery and cut into similar-sized strips. Toss the celeriac, celery, grated apple and chives together in a bowl and season with salt and pepper. Add the mayonnaise and mix well. Put to one side.

For the dressing, in a bowl, mix together the shallots, diced apple, chives, lemon juice and rapeseed oil and season with salt to taste.

Spoon the crab meat neatly onto 4 plates and pile the celeriac salad alongside. Drizzle over a few spoonfuls of the dressing and finish with some watercress. Serve the rest of the dressing in a bowl on the side.

Braised octopus with lime, olive and rocket dressing

If you have never eaten octopus before, this is a great introduction to the clever creature. Braising the fish until tender, then char-grilling the outside brings out its finest characteristics. Served simply with a lime, green olive and rocket dressing, it's delicious. I'll be surprised if you don't like it... I love it!

Serves 4
1kg octopus (double sucker species)
Olive oil for cooking
1 onion, peeled and chopped
5 garlic cloves, peeled and crushed
100ml white wine
2 thyme sprigs
Cornish sea salt and freshly ground black pepper

Lime, olive and rocket dressing
200g pitted green olives
Finely grated zest and juice of 1 lime
Large handful of rocket leaves
1 garlic clove, peeled and chopped
2 tbsp extra virgin olive oil

To finish
Finely grated zest of 1 lime
20 green olives, pitted and sliced
Handful of small rocket leaves
Extra virgin olive oil to drizzle

To braise the octopus, heat a pan large enough to hold it, and add a drizzle of oil. When the oil is hot, add the onion and garlic and cook for 2 minutes. Add the octopus, wine and thyme sprigs. Put the lid on and cook gently for 1 hour until the octopus is tender.

Remove the octopus from the pan. When cool enough to handle, slit the main body in half and remove the ink sac, stomach and eyes, then prise out the beak from the middle of the tentacles (similar to cleaning squid before cooking, see pages 208–9). Cut the tentacles and body into 4cm pieces and leave to cool.

To make the dressing, blend together the green olives, lime zest and juice, rocket leaves, garlic, extra virgin olive oil and some salt and pepper. Taste and adjust the seasoning; put to one side.

Heat a char-grill pan on a high heat. When it is hot, toss the octopus in a little olive oil, season with salt and pepper and place in the hot pan. Cook for 2 minutes, turning once or twice to colour all over.

Divide the dressing between warm plates and lay the octopus pieces on top. Scatter over the lime zest, olives and rocket leaves. Add a drizzle of extra virgin olive oil and serve immediately.

Cuttlefish braised in red wine with rosemary, mushrooms and beans

Braising fish in red wine works well for meatier species such as turbot and, for me, cuttlefish is well suited to this method too. Inspired by the hearty seafood dishes you get along the Italian coastline, this recipe is equally good with large squid.

Serves 4
2kg cuttlefish, prepared (see pages 210–11)
Light rapeseed oil for cooking
3 shallots, peeled and chopped
1 garlic bulb
2 rosemary sprigs
750ml red wine
4 tomatoes, halved
750ml fish stock (see page 213)
150g tinned (or freshly cooked) borlotti beans
100g tinned (or freshly cooked) haricot beans
100g chestnut mushrooms, quartered
Cornish sea salt and freshly ground black pepper

Gremolata
Finely grated zest of 1 lemon
Handful of flat-leaf parsley, chopped
2 garlic cloves, peeled and chopped
Extra virgin olive oil to finish

To prepare the braising liquor, heat a large saucepan and add a drizzle of oil. When it is hot, add the shallots, garlic bulb and rosemary and cook for 2 minutes. Add the wine and tomatoes, bring to the boil and reduce by half. Next, add the fish stock and bring to the boil.

Place the cuttlefish in the liquid and put a lid on the pan. Lower the heat and cook gently for 1 hour, or until tender (large cuttlefish may take longer). When the cuttlefish is cooked, remove it from the pan and set aside to cool.

Add the beans to the liquor, top up with a little water if necessary and simmer for 10 minutes. Remove and discard the garlic bulb.

Meanwhile, heat a frying pan and add a drizzle of oil. When it is hot, add the mushrooms and cook for a couple of minutes. Season with salt and pepper to taste.

Tip the mushrooms into the sauce and beans. Cut the cuttlefish into strips and add these too.

For the gremolata, mix the lemon zest, parsley and garlic together.

Share the cuttlefish, mushrooms, beans and sauce equally between 4 warm bowls. Sprinkle with the gremolata, add a drizzle of extra virgin oil and serve with chunky bread for mopping up the juices.

Braised squid 'Redas style' with pickled chicory salad

Head chef Redas Katauskas came up with this dish of tender braised squid tossed in a chervil mayo and topped with crispy squid rings. The chicory is a lovely contrast. Top drawer!

Serves 4

1kg squid, prepared and left whole (see pages 208–9)
Light rapeseed oil for cooking
2 garlic cloves, peeled
150ml white wine
2 thyme sprigs
3 tbsp mayonnaise (see page 213)
4–5 spring onions, trimmed and sliced
2 tbsp chopped chervil
150ml milk
100g semolina
Oil for deep-frying
Cornish sea salt and freshly ground black pepper

Pickled chicory salad

2 heads of chicory, trimmed
75ml white wine
75ml white wine vinegar
75ml water
75g caster sugar

To finish

Lemon oil to drizzle (see page 214)

To braise the squid, heat a medium pan and add a drizzle of oil. When it is hot, add the whole garlic cloves and cook for 1 minute. Now add the whole squid and cook for 2 minutes, turning once or twice. Season with salt and pepper, add the wine and thyme and cook gently for 5 minutes. Pour in enough water to just cover the squid, put the lid on and gently simmer for 45 minutes to 1 hour, until the squid is tender.

Drain the squid. Select 2 or 3 nice, thick ones and cut them into rings, so you have 12 rings in total; set these and the tentacles aside.

Chop the remaining squid into small dice and place in a bowl. Add the mayonnaise, spring onions, chervil and some salt and pepper. Mix well, taste for seasoning and put to one side.

To make the pickled chicory salad, separate the chicory leaves and place them in a shallow dish. Put the wine, wine vinegar, water and sugar in a pan over a medium heat to dissolve the sugar, then bring to the boil and season with salt. Pour the hot liquid over the chicory leaves and cover with a plate or cling film to keep the leaves submerged. Leave to cool.

Have the milk and semolina in two separate bowls. Dip the squid rings and tentacles, a few at a time, into the milk and then into the semolina, turning to ensure they are coated all over.

When ready to serve, heat the oil in a deep-fat fryer to 180°C. Drain the chicory, lay 6–8 leaves on each plate and pile the squid mayonnaise on top. Deep-fry the squid rings in the hot oil, in batches if necessary, for a minute until crisp. Remove and drain on kitchen paper, then season with salt and pepper. Place the squid rings next to the squid mayonnaise. Finish with a drizzle of lemon oil and serve.

Braised turbot in beer with bacon, shallots and peas

This dish, for some reason, says rich man/poor man to me. The king of the sea braised in good old beer with bacon and peas. I've portioned the turbot and cooked it on the bone, because that's how I like it, but if you've got one of those turbot kettles you could braise the whole thing. That would be cracking as well!

Serves 4

1 turbot, about 1.5kg, fins trimmed, split down the centre bone and cut into steaks with the bone in (see pages 188–9)
Light rapeseed oil for cooking
75g unsalted butter
20 small shallots, peeled
12 garlic cloves, peeled
1 rosemary sprig
100ml red wine vinegar
750ml beer (Doom Bar or other good-quality bitter)
500ml fish stock (see page 213)
8 rashers of streaky smoked bacon
200g peas (fresh or frozen)
3 tbsp flat-leaf parsley, chopped
Cornish sea salt and freshly ground black pepper

To prepare the fish braising liquid, heat a large, wide pan and add a drizzle of oil and half of the butter. When the oil is hot and the butter has melted, add the whole shallots and garlic. Cook for 4 minutes, then add the rosemary and cook for a further 2 minutes, allowing the shallots and garlic to colour slightly.

Add the wine vinegar and let it bubble until reduced to almost nothing, then pour in the beer and reduce by half. Now pour in the fish stock and bring to the boil. Skim off any impurities from the surface and simmer for 5 minutes.

Meanwhile, heat your grill to high. Lay the bacon rashers on the grill rack and grill until crispy, turning once. Leave until cool enough to handle, then chop the bacon.

To cook the fish, place the turbot portions in the beer liquor and cover with foil. Cook over a low heat for 12 minutes. Remove the foil, carefully turn the fish and add the peas and parsley. Cook for 1 minute, then take off the heat.

Carefully pour off the braising liquor into a saucepan, place over a medium heat and whisk in the remaining butter, in pieces. Pour the liquor back over the fish and scatter over the crispy bacon. Serve at once.

Other than pan-frying, grilling is probably the most popular way to cook fish. It takes little effort, after all, to pop a fish under the grill and there is nothing wrong with an easy option – some of the best seafood I've eaten and cooked has been grilled. However, it is vital to keep a close eye on your fish when it's under the grill, so that you can adjust the heat – or move the grill pan up or down – to slow down or increase the heat as you wish. In the restaurant kitchens we use salamander grills, which offer precise cooking control. If you grill a lot, you might want to consider investing in one of these – they are great to use.

Long before the invention of gas and electric grills, fish was grilled over wood or coals – as, of course, it is on a barbecue today, but I deal with that technique in the next chapter.

Before you start, it is important to heat the grill to the correct temperature for cooking. If you don't preheat your grill the skin won't colour and lightly crisp before the fish is cooked through and you'll be disappointed with the result.

Generally, a medium to medium-high heat is used, depending on the thickness and density of the fish you are cooking. For example, mackerel can handle a fairly high heat, whereas bass needs a medium heat to ensure that it cooks through to the middle before overcooking on the outside.

Size is an important consideration when you are grilling fish. A large fish will dry out on the outside before it is cooked through, so I rarely grill a whole fish that weighs more than 1kg. Filleted portions can be grilled successfully provided they are of a reasonably even thickness.

GRILLED

For me, it is pretty essential to grill fish with the skin on. The skin protects the delicate flesh from the intense heat and it is delicious to eat as it acquires a delicate crispness and slightly caramelised flavour under the grill.

I suggest you use a really strong grill tray that doesn't buckle under the heat, and oil it lightly before you add the fish. I have a favourite sturdy tray for grilling my fish, which works a treat.

I always oil and season the fish before putting it under the grill too – this helps to prevent the fish sticking to the tray. Remember that the tray remains very hot when you remove it from the heat source and will continue to cook the fish. If the fish is ready, you will need to transfer it to a warm plate or platter straight away. I normally take it from under the grill when the fish is almost there and use the heat of the tray to finish the cooking while I plate up everything else.

BEST SEAFOOD FISH FOR GRILLING

Scallops, bream (all types), dab, small gurnard, haddock, smaller John Dory, lobster, mackerel, megrim, witch, smaller plaice, Dover sole, lemon sole, prawns, red mullet, razor clams, sardines, queenie scallops, scampi.

ACCOMPANIMENTS & GARNISHES

Garlic and parsley dressing (page 124), Green sauce (page 130), seaweed butter (page 144), red pepper and saffron dressing (page 101), parsley and mustard mash (page 88), char-grilled courgettes.

Grilled plaice, asparagus and pancetta with cockles

This is a fabulous combination of flavours. At its best, plaice is as good as any other flat fish, but you must take particular care to avoid overcooking it. If you are lucky enough to get a big fat plaice, keep it on the bone and roast it whole, then bring it to the table intact so that everyone can tuck in.

Serves 4
1 large plaice, about 1kg, or 2 smaller fish, filleted (see page 185)
1kg live cockles, cleaned
150ml white wine
20 asparagus spears
2 tsp white wine shallots (see page 216)
100ml cold-pressed rapeseed oil
2 tsp chopped chives
8 thin slices of pancetta
Cornish sea salt

Place a large saucepan (that has a tight-fitting lid) over a medium heat. When hot, add the cockles and wine and put the lid on. Steam for 2 minutes until the shells open; discard any that remain closed.

Tip the contents of the pan into a colander set over a bowl to catch the cooking liquor. When the cockles are cool enough to handle, pick out the meat from the shells.

Strain the saved cooking liquor through a fine sieve (or, better still, one lined with muslin) into a small pan, to get rid of any sand from the cockles. Bring to a simmer over a medium heat and simmer until reduced by half; set aside.

Trim the asparagus and peel the lower part of the stems. Bring a pan of salted water to the boil and have ready a bowl of iced water. Add the asparagus to the boiling water and blanch for 2 minutes, then remove and drop straight into the ice-cold water to refresh. Once cooled, remove and drain. Set side until ready to serve.

To make the dressing, put the cockle meat in a large bowl and add the white wine shallots, 70ml of the rapeseed oil and the chives. Toss to mix and season with a touch of salt.

Oil the grill tray and sprinkle with salt. Lay the plaice fillets skin side up on the tray; set aside.

Heat your grill to hot. Place the pancetta on a baking tray under the grill until crispy, then remove and set aside.

Toss the asparagus spears in the remaining oil and season with a little salt.

Put the tray of plaice under the grill and cook for 5 minutes, adding the asparagus spears for the last couple of minutes, to warm and colour them all over, turning as necessary.

Meanwhile, gently heat the dressing. Add 100ml of the reserved cockle juice; don't let it boil.

Divide the grilled asparagus between warm plates and carefully lay the fish fillets skin side up on top, using a palette knife to transfer them. Add the crispy pancetta and spoon over the cockle dressing. Serve and enjoy.

Grilled red mullet on toast with tomato and saffron pickle

Fish on toast! This sort of dish should be eaten on a warm, late summer afternoon for high tea – or lunch or brunch if you prefer. Ideally, the lovely pickle will be made from tomatoes you've picked from the garden...

<u>Serves 4</u>
4 red mullet, about 200g each, scaled, gutted,
    butterflied (see pages 196–7) and pin-boned
A little light rapeseed oil for cooking
20 cherry tomatoes on the vine
Cornish sea salt

<u>Tomato and saffron pickle</u>
1 red onion, peeled and finely chopped
2 garlic cloves, peeled and finely chopped
1 tsp cumin seeds
1 red chilli, deseeded and chopped
Pinch of saffron strands
Finely grated zest of 1 lemon
500g ripe tomatoes, peeled and chopped
50g brown sugar
75ml red wine vinegar

<u>To serve</u>
4 thick slices of sourdough bread
Cold-pressed rapeseed oil to drizzle
Handful of rocket leaves

First, make the pickle. Heat a drizzle of oil in a medium pan and gently sweat the onion and garlic for 1 minute without colouring. Meanwhile, toast the cumin seeds in a small dry frying pan until fragrant. Add to the onion and garlic with the chilli, saffron and lemon zest. Continue to cook for 1 minute.

Add the tomatoes to the pan and cook over a medium heat for 10 minutes. Add the sugar and wine vinegar and cook until the mixture reaches a 'jammy' consistency; this will take about 20 minutes. Season with ½–1 tsp salt to taste and set aside to cool. (You will have more than you need for this recipe; keep the rest in the fridge and use within 4 weeks.)

To cook the fish, heat your grill to medium-high. Brush the fish with oil and season with salt, then lay skin side up on the grill tray with the cherry tomatoes. Grill for 4 minutes or until the fish is just cooked through. Don't worry if everything begins to colour – a bit of colour on the skin is good! Meanwhile, toast the bread or char on a hot griddle.

Place a slice of toast on each warm plate and spoon on some of the tomato and saffron pickle. Top with the grilled red mullet and cherry tomatoes. Add a splash of rapeseed oil to the grill tray and mix with the fish and tomato juices to make a dressing, then drizzle over the fish. Finish with a few rocket leaves. Mouth-wateringly good!

Bream with chicory tart, pink grapefruit and pistachio dressing

This was one of my earliest dishes, created at The Black Pig, my first restaurant. The combination of chicory, grapefruit and pistachios works so well and cuts the slight oiliness of the bream perfectly. And for me, grilling is the best way to cook bream, as its skin is particularly delicious when crisp and lightly charred.

Serves 4
2 bream, about 500g each, scaled, gutted, filleted and pin-boned (see pages 192–4)
A little rapeseed oil for cooking

Chicory tart
2 banana shallots, peeled and sliced
8 juniper berries, finely chopped
100ml white wine vinegar
50g unsalted butter
2 heads of chicory, trimmed and sliced
50g caster sugar
200g good-quality ready-made puff pastry
Cornish sea salt

Pistachio dressing
150g roasted and salted pistachio nuts, shelled
75ml sunflower oil

To serve
1 pink grapefruit, segmented
Handful of rocket leaves

For the chicory tart, put the shallots and juniper berries in a small pan with the wine vinegar and bring to a simmer. Let simmer until the vinegar has reduced to almost nothing. Put to one side. Heat a frying pan and add a drizzle of oil and the butter. Heat until the butter is foaming, then add the chicory and cook over a medium heat until it starts to collapse and turn translucent. Add the shallots and juniper berries, then the sugar. Cook over a medium heat for 1 minute and season with a pinch of salt. Spread the chicory on a tray and leave to cool.

Roll out your pastry on a lightly floured surface to a rough square, the thickness of a £1 coin. Place on a lined baking sheet and put in the fridge to rest for 20 minutes. Heat your oven to 180°C/Gas 4. Once rested, cover the pastry evenly with the chicory mixture and bake in the oven for 16 minutes.

While the tart is in the oven, make the pistachio dressing. Put the nuts on a board, drizzle with the sunflower oil and chop finely. Season with a touch of salt and transfer to a bowl. Once the chicory tart is cooked, allow it to cool slightly.

Heat your grill to medium-high and oil the grill tray. Lay the bream fillets skin side up on the grill tray and season with salt. Cook under the grill for about 6 minutes, depending on the thickness of the fish.

To serve, cut the chicory tart into portions. Place a wedge on each warm plate and dress with a spoonful of the pistachio dressing and a few grapefruit segments. When the fish is ready, place a portion on top. Spoon over some more dressing, add a few more grapefruit segments and scatter over the rocket leaves. Serve at once.

John Dory with curry sauce, cabbage and shallots

Using a mayonnaise-based sauce is a good way to get flavours into a dish without overpowering the taste of the fish. John Dory has a lovely delicate flavour, which is enhanced here by a subtle, fresh-tasting curry sauce. Buttery cabbage and shallots contrast the moist texture of the fish beautifully.

Serves 4
2 John Dory, about 600g each, gutted, filleted, skinned and pin-boned (see pages 192–4)
1 Savoy or hispi cabbage
75g unsalted butter
2 large banana shallots, peeled and thinly sliced
Cornish sea salt

Curry sauce
2 medium egg yolks
1 tsp mild curry powder
3 tsp white wine vinegar
200ml sunflower oil
75ml apple juice

To serve
Curry oil (see page 214)

Bring a large pan of lightly salted water to the boil. Remove and set aside 12 large outer leaves from the cabbage; halve, core and shred the rest.

Add the whole cabbage leaves to the boiling water and blanch for 2 minutes. Remove and drain thoroughly, then plunge into ice-cold water to refresh, then drain and set aside.

Heat the butter in a pan over a medium heat. When hot, add the shallots and shredded cabbage and cook for 3 minutes to soften, then tip onto a tray, spread out and leave to cool.

Lay a sheet of cling film on your work surface. Lay the cabbage leaves out on the cling film, overlapping them slightly to form a sheet. Spread the shredded cabbage and shallots evenly on top, then roll up to form a sausage and wrap tightly in the cling film, twisting the ends to secure. Pierce the cling film with the tip of a knife to release any excess water, then chill the cabbage for 2 hours.

To make the curry sauce, beat the egg yolks, curry powder, ½ tsp salt and the wine vinegar together in a bowl, then slowly whisk in the oil, drop by drop to begin with, then in a steady stream to make a smooth, thick mayonnaise. Stir in the apple juice until evenly combined, then taste and adjust the seasoning.

Heat your oven to 180°C/Gas 4. Heat your grill to its highest setting and oil a grill tray. Season the fish with salt and place skin side up on the grill tray.

Slice the cabbage roll carefully into 4 even lengths and remove the cling film. Place the cabbage rolls on a lined baking tray and warm through in the oven for 5 minutes or so.

Meanwhile, place the fish under the grill for 6 minutes or until just cooked. Gently warm the sauce in a pan until it just starts to steam, then take it off the heat and give it a good whisk.

When the fish is ready, spoon the sauce into warm deep plates. Add a cabbage roll and a fish fillet to each and finish with a drizzle of curry oil.

Scallops, hazelnut butter and watercress cream

This is a great choice for a dinner party. Not only does it look impressive, the watercress cream and hazelnut butter can be made in advance, so all you need to do is switch on the grill and cook the scallops at the last minute. I love dishes like this!

<u>Serves 4 as a starter</u>
12 medium scallops

<u>Watercress cream</u>
2 sheets of bronze leaf gelatine (4g each)
A little light rapeseed oil
1 small white onion, peeled and finely chopped
2 garlic cloves, peeled, germ removed, finely chopped
300g watercress, picked
300ml double cream

<u>Hazelnut butter</u>
150g blanched hazelnuts
1 tbsp caster sugar
100g unsalted butter, at room temperature
2 tbsp chopped flat-leaf parsley
2 tbsp chopped chives
Cornish sea salt and freshly ground black pepper

<u>To finish</u>
Handful of watercress sprigs
Olive oil for dressing

Shell and clean the scallops (see pages 206–7), removing the roes; set aside.

To make the watercress cream, soak the gelatine in a shallow dish of cold water. Heat a little oil in a medium pan and gently sweat the onion and garlic for 2 minutes without colouring. Add the watercress and sweat for another 2 minutes, then pour in the cream and let bubble for 1 minute.

Transfer the mixture to a blender. Immediately drain the gelatine leaves, squeezing out the excess water, and add them to the blender.

Blitz for 1 minute to dissolve the gelatine. Pass the mixture through a sieve into a jug and then pour into shallow soup plates. Place in the fridge for at least an hour to set.

For the hazelnut butter, toast the hazelnuts in a dry pan for about a minute until coloured and fragrant, sprinkling them with the sugar as they begin to colour. While still hot, blitz the hazelnuts in a food processor until finely ground. Let cool slightly.

While the nuts are still slightly warm, mix them with the butter and herbs and season with salt and pepper. Spoon the hazelnut butter into a sausage shape on a sheet of greaseproof paper. Cover with another sheet of paper and roll out to the thickness of a £1 coin. Chill in the freezer for 1 hour to firm up.

Using a metal cutter, cut the chilled butter into rounds, the size of the scallops. Keep in the fridge until ready to use. (You will have more than you need, so wrap the rest and freeze for another occasion.)

About 10 minutes before serving, remove the plates from the fridge to take the chill off the watercress cream. Heat your grill to medium and oil the grill tray.

Lay the scallops on the tray, season lightly with salt and grill gently for 2 minutes. Place a round of hazelnut butter on each one and grill gently for a further 2 minutes or until cooked.

To serve, arrange 3 scallops on each portion of watercress cream. Dress the handful of watercress with a little olive oil and arrange on the plates, then serve.

Scampi with burnt lime and roasted garlic and lime mayonnaise

This dish was on the original menu at my restaurant at The Capital Hotel in London. Seeing scampi (aka langoustines or Dublin Bay prawns) on a menu isn't anything new, but you are more likely to find them shelled and pan-fried. Grilling them in their shells, as I have here, gives the scampi a slightly smoky flavour, which comes from the colouring of the shells. The flavours of lime and roast garlic are the perfect match. Truly scrummy!

Serves 4
16 medium raw scampi (shell-on), live or frozen

Roasted garlic and lime mayonnaise
1 garlic bulb
250ml light rapeseed oil
2 egg yolks
1 tsp English mustard
Finely grated zest and juice of 1 lime

Garlic and parsley dressing
100ml light rapeseed oil or light olive oil
2 garlic cloves, peeled and finely chopped
1 tbsp chopped curly parsley
2 limes, halved
Cornish sea salt and freshly ground black pepper

Heat your oven to 180°C/Gas 4. For the garlic and lime mayonnaise, place the garlic bulb on a piece of foil, sprinkle with a pinch of salt and drizzle with a little of the oil. Wrap loosely in the foil and roast in the oven for 30 minutes or until soft. Unwrap the garlic bulb, then separate and peel the cloves. Mash the soft flesh until smooth or purée in a small food processor.

To make the mayonnaise, beat the egg yolks, mustard and the lime zest and juice together in a bowl, then slowly whisk in the oil, drop by drop to begin with, then in a steady stream. The mayonnaise should be thick and smooth. Stir in the garlic purée and season with salt and pepper to taste.

Place the scampi on a board and split in half lengthways from head to tail (as for lobster, see page 201). Remove the stomach and dark intestinal tract. Crack the claws and set aside. Heat your grill to high.

For the dressing, mix the 100ml oil with the chopped garlic and parsley, and a little salt and pepper. Taste for seasoning.

Place the lime halves on your grill tray and grill for a minute until coloured and golden. Add the scampi to the tray and grill for a further 5 minutes until the scampi are cooked and the lime halves are tinged with brown. There is no need to turn the scampi.

Arrange the grilled scampi and lime halves on warm plates and spoon on the garlic and parsley dressing. Serve the roasted garlic and lime mayonnaise on the side.

Barbecuing seems so straightforward – just chuck the food on the hot grid and that's it – but it isn't quite so easy, especially when it comes to cooking seafood on the barbecue.

Before you start you need to make sure your barbecue is hot enough – especially if you're cooking fish or shellfish. Personally, I don't think gas barbecues cut the mustard for seafood – they just don't get hot enough and the fish sticks. For me, barbecuing is all about cooking over coals. And the coals need to be white hot – so hot that you can't hold your hand anywhere near the grid. It's this intense heat that stops the seafood from sticking and ensures it cooks quickly and remains succulent. The coals also give seafood an incomparable flavour.

The word barbecue comes from the word *barbacoa*, which has Caribbean roots and means 'sacred fire pit'. It describes a basic grill for cooking food, consisting of a wooden platform resting on sticks over a fire. Traditionally, this involved digging a hole in the ground to take the hot coals and a cooking pot. The food was placed on the grill with the pot containing water underneath, to collect the cooking juices and produce a broth. It was then covered with leaves and coal, set alight and left to cook for a few hours. Now that might have worked for meat, but seafood cooked that way would be tough and inedible!

The best barbecued fish I've ever eaten was in a traditional seafood restaurant called Keie-Keipe in the Basque coastal town of Getaria in northern Spain. The whole fish were cooked in a specially designed clamp over coals and basted

BARBECUED

with a mixture of great olive oil and wine vinegar. As the fish rested after cooking it released the sort of magical juices that can only be created by cooking fish this way. If I can recreate anything like that I am over the moon.

I only ever barbecue whole fish on the bone – without the protection of the skin, the flesh would dry out very quickly over the intense heat. Butterflied fish work well, but I'd never cook fillets on a barbecue.

Similarly, crustaceans need to be in their shell – the flesh effectively steams within the shells and takes on the flavour from the coals without drying out.

<u>So the golden rules are:</u>
Get the coals white hot – be patient!
Cook fish with the skin on
Cook crustaceans in their shell

Only barbecue fish and shellfish that is spanking fresh, stick to the golden rules, and you will be cooking some of the tastiest seafood ever!

BEST SEAFOOD TO BARBECUE
Bass, bream, brill, grey mullet, gurnard, herring, John Dory, lobster, mackerel, monkfish, octopus, prawns, red mullet, razor clams, horse mackerel, sardines, squid, turbot, scampi, scallops.

ACCOMPANIMENTS & GARNISHES
Green sauce (page 130), roasted garlic and lime mayonnaise (page 124), anchovy, mint and coriander dressing (page 16), barbecued aubergine and courgettes, marinated tomatoes with rosemary.

Barbecued grey mullet with garlic, fennel and olives

There is something about butterflied fish cooked on a barbecue – somehow it just seems right. Lightly marinating the fish brings out its qualities and adds even more. The charred skin is really there for protection but if you get the temperature of the barbecue just right it will be lovely and crispy – delicious with the fennel, anise and garlic flavours.

Serves 4
2 grey mullet, about 1kg each, scaled, gutted, butterflied (see pages 196–7) and pin-boned
2 garlic cloves, peeled and finely chopped
Olive oil for marinating and cooking
2 medium fennel bulbs
2 red onions, peeled and quartered
Cornish sea salt and freshly ground black pepper

Black olive dressing
Handful of black olives, pitted and finely chopped
About 150ml olive oil
2 tbsp chopped dill
A splash of pastis

Salad cream
2 egg yolks
2 tsp English mustard
2 tsp caster sugar
2 tbsp lemon juice
300ml light olive oil
30ml double cream

To marinate the fish, lay the butterflied fillets on a tray, sprinkle over the garlic and season with salt and pepper. Drizzle with oil and carefully rub the flavourings into the fish. Cover and leave to marinate in the fridge for 2 hours.

Half an hour or so before the fish is required, light the barbecue.

For the salad cream, put the egg yolks, mustard, sugar and lemon juice into a blender and blitz briefly to combine. With the motor running, add the oil in a slow, steady stream. Once it is all incorporated and emulsified, transfer to a bowl, stir in the cream and season with salt and pepper to taste. Cover and chill in the fridge.

To prepare the fennel, remove any tough outer layer, then quarter the bulbs. Thread the fennel and red onion quarters onto skewers, season with salt and pepper and drizzle with oil.

For the dressing, combine all the ingredients in a bowl and season with salt and pepper.

When the barbecue coals are ready, cook the fennel and red onion skewers on a medium heat (rather than the hottest part of the barbecue) until tender; this should take about 10 minutes. Once the vegetables are cooked, take them off the barbecue and keep warm.

Now lay the butterflied fish skin side down on the hottest part of the barbecue and cook for about 4 minutes. Turn and cook for 2 minutes on the flesh side (the skin should have lifted, making it easy to turn the fish over).

Lay the fish and vegetable skewers on warm plates and spoon on the olive dressing. Serve with the salad cream.

Barbecued John Dory with green sauce and chicory

I came up with this idea when I was creating rubs for meats. Why not a rub for fish? John Dory is the perfect candidate and it cooks so well on the bone, especially on the barbecue. And the green sauce works wonders with the sweet John Dory flesh and charred chicory.

Serves 4

1 John Dory, about 2kg, or 2 smaller 1kg fish
4 heads of chicory, trimmed and leaves separated
Olive oil for cooking
Cornish sea salt and freshly ground black pepper

Spice rub

1 tbsp fennel seeds
1 tbsp black peppercorns
1 tbsp coriander seeds
1 tbsp sea salt

Green sauce

3 garlic cloves, peeled and roughly chopped
2 tbsp capers in vinegar, drained
6 good-quality salted anchovies
2 large gherkins
A handful of rocket leaves
A handful of flat-leaf parsley
½ handful of mint
1 tbsp red wine vinegar
1 tbsp English mustard
About 100ml extra virgin olive oil

Light the barbecue 30 minutes before starting to cook. To make the spice rub, toast the spices in a dry pan over a medium heat for a minute or until fragrant. Tip into a mortar, add the salt and a drizzle of oil and grind with the pestle.

Spread the spice rub over the fish, taking care – John Dory has some nasty spikes!

For the sauce, finely chop the garlic, capers, anchovies and gherkins together; put to one side. Next chop the rocket, parsley and mint together finely. Now chop the two mixtures together and place in a bowl. Stir in the wine vinegar and mustard. Add enough extra virgin olive oil to bind the mixture. Transfer the sauce to a serving bowl, cover and set aside.

Put the chicory leaves into a bowl, drizzle with olive oil, season with salt and pepper and toss to mix. Thread a large skewer through the bottom of the leaves and another, parallel, skewer through the tops, so all the leaves are held tightly on both skewers.

When ready to eat, place the chicory skewers on the barbecue and cook for about 4 minutes on each side until the leaves begin to soften and char. Move the chicory to the side of the barbecue to keep warm while you cook the fish.

Cook the fish (in a barbecue fish clamp if you have one) on the hottest part of the barbecue for 3–5 minutes without moving. Turn carefully and cook for a further 3–5 minutes until done.

Meanwhile, remove the chicory leaves from the skewers. Transfer the fish to a warm platter and arrange the chicory on the side. Serve at once, with the green sauce.

Barbecued red mullet with tomatoes, garlic and courgettes

I really like red mullet cooked this way over coals. It doesn't take long at all, so get your tomatoes and courgettes going before you put the fish on the barbecue. If you don't want to do the garlic, then just make a really herby dressing with lemon juice instead.

<u>Serves 4</u>
4 red mullet, 200–300g each, scaled, gutted, butterflied (see pages 196–7) and pin-boned
2 large beef tomatoes
2 courgettes, sliced on the diagonal
100ml olive oil
12 garlic cloves, peeled
2 rosemary sprigs, leaves only, chopped
Cornish sea salt and freshly ground black pepper

Light the barbecue about 30 minutes before starting to cook. Halve the tomatoes and place cut side up on a tray with the courgette slices. Drizzle over a little olive oil and season with salt and pepper.

Put the garlic cloves on a thick piece of foil and sprinkle with salt, pepper and the rosemary. Drizzle over the rest of the olive oil and scrunch up the foil around the garlic to make a parcel; seal well. Place on the cooler side of the barbecue to cook slowly for about 25 minutes.

Place the tomato halves cut side down and the courgette slices on the hot part of the barbecue for 3 minutes, then turn and cook for a further 3 minutes. When they begin to soften, move them to the cooler area of the barbecue and allow to cook through.

Check the garlic: the cloves should be soft when you pinch them. When it is ready, pour the contents of the foil packet onto a tray and allow to cool slightly.

Lay the red mullet on the same tray and spoon over the cooked garlic and rosemary mixture, then season with salt and pepper.

Now place the butterflied fish skin side down on the hottest part of the barbecue and cook for about 4 minutes. Turn and cook for 2 minutes on the flesh side.

Divide the roasted garlic cloves between the tomato halves and dress with a spoonful of the rosemary oil.

Carefully lift the red mullet from the barbecue onto a warm platter and add the tomato halves and courgettes. Drizzle over the remaining garlic and rosemary oil and serve.

Seafood burger with charred baby gem and wasabi mayonnaise

My fish burger has become a firm favourite at my new restaurant, Outlaw's Fish Kitchen in Port Isaac. This is a variation on the original recipe which appeared in my first book. Spiked with chilli and served with wasabi mayonnaise, it has a lovely fiery kick.

Serves 4
100g fresh crab meat (mixed white and brown)
100g shelled prawns, deveined
200g cod fillet, skinned and pin-boned
A little olive oil for cooking
2 shallots, peeled and finely chopped
2 garlic cloves, peeled and finely chopped
1 green chilli, deseeded and finely chopped
Cornish sea salt and freshly ground black pepper

Wasabi mayonnaise
2 egg yolks
2 tbsp lemon juice
300ml sunflower oil
50g freshly grated English wasabi or paste
3 tsp chopped wasabi leaf, if available

To serve
2 baby gem lettuces, trimmed
Burger buns (see page 218), split
Pickled onions (see page 216)

Pick over the crab meat, checking for fragments of shell or cartilage and place in a large bowl. Roughly chop the prawns and cod.

Heat a frying pan over a medium heat and add a little olive oil. When hot, add the shallots, garlic and chilli and cook for 2 minutes without colouring. Tip onto a plate and leave to cool.

Put the cod into a blender and pulse for 20–30 seconds; it should have some texture rather than be smooth. Add the fish to the crab meat and stir to combine. Add the chopped prawns together with the cooled shallot mixture and mix well, seasoning with salt and pepper.

Divide the mixture into 4 equal portions and mould them into patties. Place on a tray and chill in the fridge for 30 minutes.

Now light the barbecue. While it is heating up, make the mayonnaise. Put the egg yolks and lemon juice into a bowl and whisk to combine. Continuing to whisk, add the oil, drop by drop to begin with, then in a steady stream until it is all incorporated and the mayonnaise is thick. Add the grated wasabi, stirring it through thoroughly. Season with salt to taste and add the wasabi leaf, if using.

When ready to cook, thread the baby gem lettuces onto a large skewer. Place the patties on the barbecue for 3 minutes, then turn and cook for a further 3 minutes. As you turn them, add the skewer and char the lettuce on both sides. At the same time, toast the burger buns on the barbecue grid.

To assemble, place a couple of baby gem leaves on the bottom half of each burger bun with some pickled onions, then top with the patties. Add a generous dollop of wasabi mayonnaise. Sandwich together with the bun tops and serve.

Barbecued chilli squid and aubergine with ginger and coriander yoghurt

Squid works so well with Asian flavours and it's great cooked quickly on the barbecue. The spiced aubergine is cracking with it and it's all cooled by the ginger and coriander yoghurt.

Serves 4

8 squid, about 100g each, prepared – tubes and
   tentacles whole, wings scored (see pages 208–9)
2 red chillies, deseeded and chopped
50g root ginger, peeled and chopped
2 shallots, peeled and chopped
3 garlic cloves, peeled and chopped
3 tbsp fish sauce
40ml water
2 aubergines, halved lengthways
Olive oil for cooking and dressing
1 tsp ground coriander
1 tsp ground cumin
2 tsp chopped thyme leaves
Cornish sea salt

Ginger and coriander yoghurt

150g root ginger, peeled
200ml Greek-style natural yoghurt
3 tsp chopped coriander (optional, but preferable)

To finish

Coriander sprigs

To make the chilli paste, put the chillies, ginger, shallots, garlic and fish sauce into a blender and blend until fine. Scrape down the sides of the blender and add the water with a pinch of salt. Blend for a couple of minutes to a paste.

Place the squid in a bowl, add the chilli paste and turn the squid to coat in the paste. Leave to marinate in a cool place for at least 2 hours.

Light the barbecue 30 minutes before starting to cook.

Meanwhile, for the yoghurt, blitz the ginger in a blender to a pulp, then tip into a piece of muslin, gather up the edges and squeeze tightly over a bowl to extract the juice; you need 3 tbsp ginger juice. Add the yoghurt and coriander, if using, season with a pinch of salt and stir to mix.

Score the cut side of the aubergine halves and drizzle with 3 tbsp olive oil, then season with salt and the ground coriander and cumin.

When the barbecue coals are ready, place the aubergine halves skin side down on the grid and cook for 6 minutes, then turn over and cook for another 6 minutes to blacken the flesh. Turn the aubergine back onto the skin side again, and drizzle again with olive oil and a pinch of salt. Cook for another 4 minutes, then remove from the heat.

Scrape the cooked aubergine out of the skin and into a bowl. Crush it with the back of a fork or spoon and taste for seasoning. Dress with olive oil, sprinkle with chopped thyme and keep warm at the side of the barbecue.

To cook the squid, place it on the barbecue and cook for 1 minute on each side. Transfer to a warm platter and spoon the aubergine alongside. Serve immediately, with the yoghurt and a scattering of coriander.

Scallop and red onion skewers with sweetcorn chutney

For a special occasion, I love to cook scallops on the barbecue, they are just so delicious cooked this way. The sweetcorn chutney goes well with all sorts of things, including cold meats, so refrigerate any you have left over. Make sure your barbecue is white hot for these skewers – if it's not hot enough the food will stick.

Serves 4

20 medium scallops
2 red onions, peeled
A bunch of basil, leaves picked
Cornish sea salt and freshly ground black pepper

Sweetcorn chutney

4 sweetcorn cobs, husks removed
2 red peppers, deseeded and diced
1 red chilli, deseeded and finely chopped
2 red onions, peeled and finely chopped
450ml cider vinegar
200g caster sugar
3 tsp wholegrain mustard
A pinch of saffron strands

To make the sweetcorn chutney, bring a pan of water to the boil, add some salt and the corn cobs and boil for 2 minutes. Drain and leave until cool enough to handle, then cut the sweetcorn kernels from the cobs.

Put the sweetcorn kernels in a saucepan with 1 tsp salt and the rest of the chutney ingredients. Bring to the boil, lower the heat and simmer for about 15 minutes, stirring occasionally. The consistency should be slightly wetter than a chutney. Taste for seasoning, adding more salt if required.

Shell and clean the scallops (see pages 206–7), removing the roes. Cut the onions into quarters and separate the layers into individual petals. Thread the scallops, red onion petals and basil leaves alternately onto 4 long metal skewers. You should have 5 scallops on each one skewer. Place in the fridge to chill.

Light the barbecue 30 minutes before starting to cook. Take the scallop kebabs from the fridge, season them with salt and pepper and drizzle with oil. Place the scallops on the barbecue and cook for 4 minutes, giving each one a quarter-turn every minute. Serve immediately on warm plates, with a spoonful of sweetcorn chutney on the side.

There are several different ways of baking fish, from simply roasting it whole on the bone – dotted with butter and herbs – to cooking it in a tart or pie. It's important to protect the fish from the dry heat of the oven but there are lots of ways of doing this. If you are baking a whole fish, leave it on the bone with the skin on and baste it with melted butter or oil a few times during cooking to keep it moist. In a pie, the fish is kept succulent within a sauce under the pastry or mashed potato crust.

We naturally think of baking as an oven method, but fish can also be baked using hot ashes, hot stones and wood-burning ovens, as it was in times past. Baking is very closely related to barbecuing. As far back as the ancient Egyptians and Greeks,

brick or stone-built ovens and smoke pits were used, which are similar to using a barbecue. Even then, it was understood that the fish needed protection from the heat and it was often wrapped in leaves or seaweed, or baked in a salt or dough crust.

We still use these techniques today. Baking in a salt crust is a great way to cook whole bass or bream. You simply enclose the fish in a thick layer of salt and spray it with water before it goes in the oven. The salt forms a crust, which seals in the fish, keeping in its flavour and moisture. The crust is broken and removed before serving. Cooking fish such as salmon and sea trout *en croûte* (in pastry) also works well.

One of the simplest ways to protect fish – whole or fillets – is to wrap them

BAKED

in foil with a little liquid, such as wine, some herbs and a few aromatics, like onion and garlic. Effectively the fish steams in the sealed package and stays deliciously moist.

Similarly fish fillets can be cooked *en papillote* – in baking parchment or greaseproof paper parcels. This is a really nice way to bake fish, using different herbs, liquids and vegetables in the bag with the fish. When I cook fish this way I open the parcels at the table so guests can savour all the delicious aromas as they are released. A little bit of culinary theatre!

And where would we be without the all-time classic fish pie? It can take leftover fish and shellfish, or it can be made with a medley of luxury seafood. A huge fish pie is a great choice for a party, not least

because it is quite forgiving. Bathed in its sauce, the fish won't dry out if you leave the pie to stand for a short while. A true vehicle for flavour!

BEST SEAFOOD FOR BAKING
Scallops (in the shell), bass, bream and grey mullet (in a salt crust), turbot (in the bag), plaice, stuffed trout, lobster, all sorts in pies.

ACCOMPANIMENTS & GARNISHES
Green sauce (page 130), tomato ketchup (page 215), classic parsley sauce, tarragon and anchovy butter (page 142), seaweed butter (page 144), beetroot and watercress salad (page 150).

Baked whole plaice and cider onions with tarragon and anchovy butter

I really wanted to get this recipe into my first book but I couldn't fit it in, so I'm delighted to find a place for it here (ha, ha!). Plaice is one of those fish that doesn't get enough praise. At its best, it is unbeatable in my view. It can handle all sorts of flavours – cider, tarragon, anchovy and onions for instance!

Serves 2
1 plaice, at least 1kg, gutted
50ml olive oil
2 white onions, peeled and finely sliced
2 bay leaves
200ml dry cider
Cornish sea salt and freshly ground black pepper

Tarragon and anchovy butter
200g unsalted butter, softened
Bunch of tarragon, leaves only
2 shallots, peeled and finely chopped
4 salted anchovy fillets, chopped

To serve
Lemon wedges

Heat your oven to 220°C/Gas 7.

For the flavoured butter, put the softened butter into a bowl. Chop the tarragon and add to the butter with the chopped shallots and anchovies. Mix well until evenly combined and season with pepper, and a little salt, if needed, to taste. Shape the butter into a roll on a sheet of cling film, wrap in the film and twist and tie the ends to seal. Refrigerate to firm up.

Put the olive oil, onions and bay leaves in a roasting tray, pour on the cider and cook in the oven for 20 minutes.

Season the plaice all over with salt and pepper. Take the roasting tray from the oven and lay the fish on top of the onions. Put the tray back in the oven and cook for 12–15 minutes, or until the plaice is just cooked.

Meanwhile, unwrap and slice the butter. To check the fish is cooked, make an incision into the thickest part and see if the flesh is pulling away from the bone.

Slice the butter, lay it on top of the fish and pop the tray back into the oven for 2 minutes.

Serve the plaice simply with the cider onions and lemon wedges.

Turbot steak with seaweed butter, turnips and potatoes

Turbot baked on the bone – it's such a lovely way of cooking this fish. All the natural juices from the fish cook into the potatoes and turnips with the rich, ozoney and zesty flavours from the seaweed butter. So tasty!

<u>Serves 2</u>
2 turbot steaks, about 250g each
2 large baking potatoes, peeled
2 small turnips, peeled
3 shallots, peeled and sliced
2 garlic cloves, peeled and chopped
2 tsp thyme leaves, chopped
Juice of 1 lemon
250ml fish stock (see page 213)
A little light rapeseed oil for cooking

<u>Seaweed butter</u>
250g unsalted butter, softened
3 tbsp dried sea lettuce
1 shallot, peeled and finely chopped
2 garlic cloves, peeled and finely chopped
Finely grated zest of 1 lemon
Cornish sea salt and freshly ground black pepper

Heat your oven to 200°C/Gas 6.

To make the flavoured butter, put the softened butter into a bowl and add the seaweed, shallot, garlic and lemon zest. Mix well until evenly combined and season with salt and pepper. Shape the butter into a roll on a sheet of cling film, wrap in the film and twist and tie the ends to seal. Refrigerate to firm up.

Cut the potatoes and turnips into fine slices, 2–3mm thick, using a sharp knife or mandoline. Lay them evenly in a baking dish (large enough to hold the fish) and scatter over the shallots, garlic and thyme. Season with salt and pepper, sprinkle with the lemon juice and pour on the fish stock. Bake in the oven for 45 minutes or until the potatoes are just cooked.

About 5 minutes before the potatoes will be ready, heat a frying pan over a medium heat and add a little oil. When it is hot, add the turbot steaks and pan-fry them for about a minute on each side, just enough to lightly colour the flesh. Take the baking dish from the oven. Season the turbot steaks with salt and pepper and lay them on top of the potatoes. Place the dish back in the oven for 10 minutes.

Meanwhile, slice the butter, allowing 3 slices per portion. Place the butter on top of the turbot steaks and bake for another 2 minutes. Serve at once, with a green vegetable or salad.

Bacon-wrapped trout with oyster stuffing and cucumber chutney

Fresh trout – typically served with almonds, green beans and brown butter – was the 70s restaurant scene staple menu headliner. It is often overlooked these days but an oyster stuffing works brilliantly with it, especially when the fish is wrapped in bacon. I like to think this dish helps out the uncool trout.

<u>Serves 2</u>
2 trout, 300–400g each, scaled, gutted and rinsed
16 rashers of smoked streaky bacon or pancetta
A little olive oil for cooking
Cornish sea salt and freshly ground black pepper

<u>Stuffing</u>
12 live Pacific oysters
75g unsalted butter
2 shallots, peeled and finely chopped
2 garlic cloves, peeled and finely chopped
100g breadcrumbs
Finely grated zest and juice of 1 lemon
1½ tbsp chervil leaves, chopped
1½ tbsp dill leaves, chopped

<u>Cucumber chutney</u>
1 cucumber
½ green chilli, deseeded and chopped
1 shallot, peeled and finely chopped
1 garlic clove, peeled and finely chopped
50ml white wine vinegar
50g caster sugar
1 tsp mustard seeds
1½ tbsp chervil leaves, chopped
1½ tbsp dill leaves, chopped

Heat your oven to 200°C/Gas 6. For the stuffing, open the oysters (see page 204) and strain their juice through a muslin-lined sieve into a bowl.

Chop the oysters and add them to the bowl. Heat a small pan over a medium heat and add the butter. When it is bubbling, add the shallots and garlic and cook for 1 minute, without colouring. Tip into a bowl and let cool slightly. Mix in the breadcrumbs, lemon zest, chopped herbs, oysters and their juice. Season with salt and pepper to taste.

Lay half of the bacon rashers, side by side, on a work surface to form a sheet and place one trout, skin side down, across them. Repeat with the remaining bacon and trout. Season the fish with salt and pepper. Divide the stuffing equally between them, then fold back to their natural shape, enclosing the stuffing, and wrap the bacon around them. Place the trout join side down on one or two baking trays. Drizzle with a little olive oil and bake in the oven for about 20 minutes until cooked through.

While the fish is in the oven, make the chutney. Grate the cucumber into a bowl, then take it out and squeeze it in your hands to remove excess water. Put the cucumber back into the bowl and add the chilli, shallot and garlic. Heat the wine vinegar, sugar and mustard seeds in a small pan to dissolve the sugar, then pour over the cucumber mixture. Let cool slightly, then add the chopped herbs and season with salt and pepper to taste.

When the fish are cooked, lift them onto warm plates. Serve the cucumber chutney on the side.

Starrey gazey pies

Originating from Mousehole in Cornwall, this pie is traditionally eaten in the village on the eve of December 23rd, the festival of Tom Bawcock. It celebrates his heroic catch for the small fishing village in very stormy winter to prevent the villagers from starving. My recipe – for individual pies rather than a big one – uses mackerel rather than pilchards and leaves out the traditional potato and egg.

Serves 4

4 medium mackerel, gutted and butterflied, tails intact (see pages 196–7)

Pastry

250g plain flour, plus extra to dust
1 tsp fine sea salt
250g very cold butter, cut into cubes
About 125ml ice-cold water
Egg wash (1 egg yolk beaten with 2 tsp milk)

Filling

50ml light rapeseed oil
3 rashers of smoked streaky bacon, derinded and diced
2 shallots, peeled and chopped
2 garlic cloves, peeled and chopped
40g plain flour
50ml cider vinegar
100ml cider
100ml fish stock (see page 213)
150g hog's pudding, diced
3 tsp chopped chives
Cornish sea salt and freshly ground black pepper

To make the pastry, combine the flour and salt in a bowl. Add the butter and rub in using your fingertips, until the butter cubes are smaller and the dough is grainy. Add enough water, a little at a time, to bring the dough together. Roll the dough into a ball, wrap in cling film and chill in the fridge for 20 minutes.

Roll out the pastry on a lightly floured surface to a rectangle, about 30 x 20cm. Fold into three, as if folding a letter to go into an envelope.

Turn the pastry 90° and roll out and fold as before, then wrap the pastry in cling film and chill for 30 minutes. Repeat the same two roll, fold and turns once more, then wrap and chill for a further 30 minutes. The pastry is now ready to roll.

To make the filling, heat a saucepan over a medium heat and add the oil. When hot, add the diced bacon and cook for 4 minutes until golden. Add the shallots and garlic and cook for 2 minutes, stirring occasionally. Add the flour and cook, stirring, for a further 2 minutes. Now gradually add the cider vinegar, cider and fish stock, stirring as you go. Bring to the boil, lower the heat and simmer for 5 minutes, stirring occasionally to ensure it does not catch.

Add the hog's pudding and chives, then take off the heat. Season with salt and pepper and divide between 4 individual pie dishes. Clean the edges of the dishes and leave to cool.

Roll out the pastry into 4 ovals or rounds (large enough to cover the pie dishes) and put back into the fridge for 10 minutes to firm up. Heat your oven to 200°C/Gas 6.

Cut the tails from the mackerel and set aside. Check the fish for any pin bones and season with salt and pepper. Lay the fillets on top of the cooled filling. Brush the rims of the dishes with egg wash and position the pastry lids over the filling. Trim away excess pastry but don't be too tidy – you're after a rustic look! Place them in the fridge until ready to cook.

Bake the pies for 15–20 minutes until the pastry is golden. Cut a hole in the top of each pie and insert a fish tail. Pop back into the oven for 5 minutes, then serve immediately, with a green salad or vegetables.

Smoked mackerel, goat's cheese and beetroot tart

I'm a fan of quiche-style fish tarts – they are such a great baked vehicle for interesting fillings – and this one is one of my favourites. You can make a big tart if you prefer, but these look so good and they're perfect for a picnic.

Serves 4

Pastry
250g plain flour, plus extra to dust
150g unsalted butter, diced
1 tsp fine sea salt
2 tsp thyme leaves, chopped
1 egg, beaten
1 tbsp cold milk
Egg wash (1 egg yolk beaten with 2 tsp milk)

Filling
3 eggs
150ml double cream
1 tbsp creamed horseradish
150ml beetroot juice
150g smoked mackerel, flaked
50g firm goat's cheese, crumbled
1½ tbsp chopped dill
Cornish sea salt and freshly ground black pepper

Beetroot and watercress salad
300g raw beetroot, peeled and finely shredded
2 tbsp sherry vinegar
75ml extra virgin olive oil
2 handfuls of watercress

To serve
Lemon wedges

To make the pastry, put the flour, butter, salt and thyme into a food processor and process until the mixture resembles fine breadcrumbs.

Add the egg and milk and pulse briefly until the dough comes together. Shape the pastry into a disc, wrap in cling film and rest in the fridge for 1 hour.

Heat your oven to 200°C/Gas 6. Roll out the rested pastry on a lightly floured surface to the thickness of a £1 coin and use to line four 10cm loose-based individual flan tins, 2cm deep. Line the pastry cases with a disc of greaseproof paper and add a layer of baking beans. Chill for 10 minutes.

Bake the pastry cases for 15 minutes, then lift out the paper and baking beans and brush the pastry with egg wash. Turn the oven down to 160°C/Gas 3.

For the filling, lightly beat the eggs, cream, horseradish and beetroot juice together in a bowl and season with salt and pepper. Scatter the smoked mackerel, goat's cheese and dill evenly into the pastry cases, then pour over the egg mixture. Bake for 20 minutes, until the custard is set and the pastry is golden.

Meanwhile, for the salad, mix the beetroot, sherry vinegar and extra virgin oil together in a bowl and season with salt and pepper to taste.

When the tarts are ready, leave them to stand for 5 minutes or so, to cool slightly. Add the watercress to the beetroot and toss to mix. Place a tart on each plate and arrange a pile of salad alongside. Serve with lemon wedges.

Spider crab omelette

This is a great 'quick and easy' recipe that can be served in the best of restaurants, or eaten at home on your lap, which is my favourite way to enjoy it! Spider crab is delicious and works so well with tomatoes and white wine. These awesome creatures are easy to catch during the summer, but if you have difficulty sourcing one, you can use brown crab, lobster or any other seafood instead. You can either make one big omelette to share or individual ones if you have small omelette pans.

Serves 4
280g picked, cooked spider crab meat
   (see pages 202–3)
A little light rapeseed oil for cooking
1 banana shallot, peeled and chopped
1 garlic clove, peeled and chopped
½ red chilli, deseeded and chopped
2 plum tomatoes, chopped
100ml white wine
100g cream cheese
200ml double cream
8 large free-range eggs, plus 2 egg yolks
   for the glaze
2 tsp chopped flat-leaf parsley
50g unsalted butter, cut into 4 pieces
80g Parmesan, freshly grated
Cornish sea salt and freshly ground black pepper

Heat your oven to 200°C/Gas 6. Heat a small pan over a medium heat and add a drizzle of oil. When it is hot, add the shallot, garlic and chilli and cook for 1 minute, without colouring.

Add the tomatoes, lower the heat and cook for 4 minutes until they start to break down. Now add the wine and bring to a simmer. Cook until the liquid has reduced right down, to almost nothing. Season with salt and pepper to taste, then transfer the mixture to a bowl and leave to cool. Once cooled, add the crab meat and mix well. Check the seasoning and set aside.

Beat the cream cheese, cream, 2 egg yolks and chopped parsley together in a bowl to make the glaze. Season with salt and pepper and set aside.

Preheat your grill. Whisk the 8 eggs together in a large bowl with a fork. Heat a large ovenproof frying pan (or 4 individual pans) over a medium heat (not too hot!) and add the butter. As soon as it has melted, pour in the egg (dividing it evenly if using individual pans) and cook lightly for 45 seconds; the egg will still be very runny, which is fine!

Remove the pan(s) from the heat and add the crab meat, scattering it evenly over the egg. Place the pan(s) in the oven for 4 minutes (or 2 minutes for individual ones). Remove from the oven and spoon over the glaze mixture, then sprinkle with the Parmesan. Put back in the oven for 4 minutes (or 3 minutes for individual ones). Finally, pop under the grill for a minute or two, until the glaze is bubbling and golden. Serve immediately.

This is probably the most common of all seafood cooking techniques, but is also the most abused. The history of fish cooking is littered with overcooked pan-fried fish! Not surprisingly perhaps, it is so easily done.

It takes no time to pan-fry a fillet of fish, so make sure you have everything else – sauce, garnishes and accompaniments – prepared before you begin and don't start cooking until your guests are ready to eat. Another potential pitfall is to fry your fish in a pan that is too hot – you need a medium rather than a high heat.

Nowadays there is a variety of pans to choose from, including cast-iron, stainless steel and ceramic, with or without a non-stick surface. For me, a good-quality non-stick pan is the way to go. Buy the best you can afford – a good-quality non-stick pan is a pleasure to use and will last a lot longer.

Fish fillets, with skin, lend themselves well to pan-frying. Always do most of the cooking on the skin side, as this acts as a protective layer, keeping the flesh moist and succulent. If you're pan-frying skinless fillets, you'll need to be very careful. Thin fillets, in particular, will dry out quickly in a hot pan and are really better steamed or grilled briefly.

The most important stage of pan-frying for me is when you turn the fish over. I fry the fish fillets skin side down until the flesh is still slightly opaque in the middle, then turn off the heat and turn the fish over so the skin side is uppermost. There is no need to turn the heat back on – the fish

PAN-FRIED

will finish off cooking in the residual heat of the pan. This slow finish of the cooking will give you time to plate up your garnish, sauce and any accompaniments.

The other great thing about pan-frying is all the lovely juices and oils that are released by the fish as you cook it. Once you've removed the seafood, add a splash of wine to the pan to deglaze it, stirring to lift all that flavour in the sediment. Now add a few softened shallots and a touch of cream, simmer for a minute, then add some herbs and there you have it – a simple pan sauce.

What I like most about pan-frying is the speed and convenience. Scallops, squid and most fillets of fish will cook in minutes in a frying pan – quicker than any microwave meal would take to heat up. If you have a good fishmonger or other source of seafood available to you, pan-frying allows you to rustle up a seafood lunch or dinner in next to no time.

BEST SEAFOOD TO PAN-FRY
Scallops, bream (all types), grey mullet, hake, gurnard, haddock, John Dory, red mullet, squid, scampi.

ACCOMPANIMENTS & GARNISHES
Tomato and anchovy (or olive) dressing (page 170), herb mayonnaise (page 213), sautéed mushrooms with garlic and parsley (page 159), crushed peas, broad beans and mint, grilled peppers with thyme oil.

Gurnard with caramelised chicory and orange

There are several varieties of gurnard, but the most popular are the red, grey and the larger tub. This dish works best with the smaller red gurnard, which cook quickly and more evenly. Their sweet taste works well with the bitter chicory and orange, and the mustard adds a kick. Be warned, the scales on small gurnard can be difficult to remove, so you may need to skin the fillets to lose them, or leave them on.

Serves 4

4 gurnard, about 600g each, scaled, gutted,
    filleted and pin-boned
3 heads of white chicory
Light rapeseed oil for cooking
1 red onion, peeled and sliced
2 tsp chopped chervil
2 tsp chopped tarragon
2 tsp Dijon mustard
200g full-fat crème fraîche
2 heads of red chicory
2 oranges
3 tbsp caster sugar
100g unsalted butter
Cornish sea salt and freshly ground black pepper

For the chicory, heat up your steamer (or, better still, use a Chinese bamboo steamer over a pan of simmering water). Halve 2 white chicory heads lengthways and season with a little salt. Cook them in the steamer for 10 minutes.

Meanwhile, heat a small frying pan over a medium heat and add a little oil. When hot, add the onion and cook for 2 minutes, without colouring. Season with salt and pepper, remove from the pan and leave to cool.

In a small bowl, stir the herbs and mustard into the crème fraîche. Season with salt and pepper to taste.

Slice the remaining white chicory and the red chicory and place in a bowl. Add the cooled onion and enough of the crème fraîche to dress the chicory.

Finely grate the zest and squeeze the juice from one of the oranges; segment the other orange, cut into small pieces and set aside.

Remove the steamed chicory from the steamer. Heat a large frying pan over a medium heat and add the sugar. When it starts to caramelise, add the steamed chicory halves, cut side down, and caramelise for 1 minute without turning. Add half of the butter with the orange zest and juice. Let bubble until the liquor starts to thicken, then remove from the heat. Transfer the chicory to a warm plate and keep warm.

Wipe out the pan and return to a medium heat. When hot, add a drizzle of oil. Season the fish fillets all over and then place skin side down in the pan. Cook for 3 minutes, then turn the fish over and add the remaining butter. Reduce the heat to low and cook gently for another couple of minutes.

Place a caramelised chicory half on each plate with a portion of the creamy dressed chicory and onion. Arrange the pan-fried gurnard fillets on the plates and finish with the orange pieces. Serve at once.

Grey mullet with mushrooms and saffron and roasted garlic potato purée

Grey mullet, at its best, is one of my favourite fish. The fish caught out at sea are sometimes compared to bass, but to me this fish has its own unique flavour and texture. One thing for sure, it can handle some big flavours, so garlic, saffron, mushrooms and parsley work very well with it. Why pan-fried? You wait until you taste that skin, then you'll get it!

Serves 4
4 grey mullet fillets, about 200g each, pin-boned
Cornish sea salt and freshly ground black pepper

Saffron and roasted garlic potato purée
1 large garlic bulb
150ml light olive oil, plus extra for cooking
500g floury potatoes, peeled (300g peeled weight)
½ tsp saffron strands
4 egg yolks
50ml white wine vinegar

Sautéed mushrooms with garlic and parsley
1 garlic clove (from above), peeled
A handful of flat-leaf parsley, chopped
300g mixed wild or Japanese-style cultivated
    mushrooms

To serve
Good-quality olive oil for dressing
2 limes, halved

Heat your oven to 200°C/Gas 6. Split the garlic bulb into individual cloves. Take a square of foil and scrunch up the sides. Put all but one of the garlic cloves inside, sprinkle with salt and drizzle with a little olive oil. Seal the foil bag, place on an oven tray and roast for 20 minutes.

Meanwhile, put the potatoes into a pan of cold salted water, bring to a simmer and cook until soft, about 15 minutes. Drain and leave in the colander to dry for a few minutes.

Let the roasted garlic cool slightly, then peel. Put the potatoes in a food processor with the saffron, roasted garlic and egg yolks and blend, adding the 150ml olive oil in a steady stream. When it is all incorporated, stop the machine and add the wine vinegar and a little salt. Blend for 2 minutes, then taste and adjust the seasoning. Transfer to a bowl, cover with cling film and keep warm until ready to serve.

Heat an ovenproof non-stick frying pan (or one that doesn't stick) over a medium heat. Chop the reserved garlic clove with the parsley. When the pan is hot, add a drizzle of olive oil, then the mushrooms. Cook for 2 minutes, seasoning with salt and pepper. Add the chopped garlic and parsley and stir well. Transfer the mushrooms to a dish; keep warm.

Wipe out the pan and return to a medium heat. When hot, add a drizzle of oil. Season the fish all over with salt and pepper and place skin side down in the pan. Cook for about 3 minutes until the edges start to turn golden, then transfer to the oven for 2 minutes.

As you remove the frying pan from the oven, turn the fish fillets over; the residual heat in the pan will finish the cooking while you start to plate up.

Share the mushrooms between 4 warm plates and put a large spoonful of the potato purée alongside. Add a pan-fried fish fillet, placing it skin side up, and finish with a drizzle of good olive oil and a lime half.

Hake with cabbage, squash and angels on horseback

Angels on horseback: how cool does that sound? Our ancestors knew how to finish a party in style with a few drinks and a platter of these. Here I've used them to add an extra dimension to a simple hake dish. That burst of smoky, salty bacon and the light ozone aroma of the oyster work so well with the mild-flavoured fish. Pan-fried slices of squash and buttery Savoy cabbage are perfect partners.

Serves 4
4 hake fillet portions, about 200g each, scaled, filleted and pin-boned
8 Pacific oysters
8 rashers of pancetta or smoked streaky bacon
2 large handfuls of shredded Savoy cabbage
Light olive oil for cooking
4 thick slices of squash
2 shallots, peeled and chopped
1 garlic clove, peeled and chopped
50g unsalted butter

Thyme dressing
150ml good-quality olive oil
4 tbsp white wine vinegar
1 tsp thyme leaves
Cornish sea salt and freshly ground black pepper

Heat your oven to 200°C/Gas 6. Open the oysters (see page 204) and strain off their juice through a muslin-lined sieve into a bowl. Wrap each oyster in a rasher of bacon and set aside.

Blanch the cabbage in boiling salted water for 2 minutes, refresh in ice-cold water, then drain.

Heat a frying pan over a medium heat and add a drizzle of olive oil. When hot, add the squash slices and cook for 2 minutes until coloured, then turn and cook for a minute on the other side. Place in a large oven dish (that will also hold the fish) and season with salt and pepper.

Heat a non-stick frying pan over a medium heat and add a drizzle of oil. Season the fish all over with salt and place skin side down in the pan. Cook for about 3 minutes until the skin is golden, then transfer to the oven dish with the squash. Place in the oven to cook for 5 minutes.

Meanwhile, wipe the pan clean and heat it up again. When hot, add a drizzle of oil, then the bacon-wrapped oysters and colour them all over for 2 minutes. Remove and keep warm.

Add the shallots and garlic to the pan and cook for 30 seconds, then add the butter. When it bubbles, add the blanched cabbage, season with salt and pepper and toss over the heat for 1 minute, then drain.

For the dressing, mix the olive oil, wine vinegar and thyme together until evenly blended, and season with salt and pepper to taste.

Spoon the cabbage onto warm plates and place the hake portions on top. Add a slice of squash to each plate and top with two angels on horseback. Trickle over the dressing and serve.

Squid, chorizo and tomatoes on ink toast with lemon yoghurt

Pan-fried squid is brilliant for a quick meal: 2 minutes in a hot pan and it's done. This invigorating dish has lots of zingy flavours, a spicy hit from the chorizo and contrasting textures too – just the thing for a fast, hearty lunch. Yummy! I'd even eat it for breakfast.

Serves 4

600g prepared squid – bodies whole, wings scored and tentacles cut individually (see pages 208–9)
Light olive oil for cooking
4–6 ripe plum tomatoes, halved lengthways
2 shallots, peeled and cut into rings
2 garlic cloves, peeled and finely sliced
1 tsp thyme leaves
About 180g cooking chorizo, cut into 12 slices
200g tinned tomatoes

Lemon yoghurt

200ml thick Greek yoghurt
Finely grated zest and juice of 1 lemon
Cornish sea salt and freshly ground black pepper

To serve

4 slices of squid ink bread (see page 219),
    or other good rustic bread
1 lemon, cut into wedges

Heat a large frying pan over a medium heat and add a drizzle of olive oil. When hot, add the plum tomatoes cut side down, season with salt and pepper and cook for 3 minutes. Turn the tomatoes over and add the shallots, garlic, thyme and chorizo to the pan. Reduce the heat to low and sweat for about 3 minutes.

Meanwhile, briefly blitz the tinned tomatoes in a blender to a pulp. Tip into the pan, bring to a simmer and cook gently until the fresh plum tomatoes start to collapse, but still hold their shape. Using a slotted spoon, remove these from the pan and set aside on a plate. Continue to simmer the sauce until it is thick.

For the lemon yoghurt, in a bowl, mix the thick yoghurt with the lemon zest and 1 tbsp lemon juice. Season with salt and pepper to taste and put to one side.

Toast the slices of bread; keep warm.

Set a large non-stick frying pan over a medium-high heat and add a drizzle of oil. Season the squid with salt and plenty of pepper. When the pan is hot, add the squid and spread it out to ensure all the pieces are in contact with the pan. Cook for 1 minute, turn it over, count to 20, then remove from the pan.

Place a piece of toast on each warm plate and add 2 or 3 plum tomato halves. Spoon on the chorizo and tomato sauce and share the squid between the plates. Serve a dollop of the lemon yoghurt and a wedge of lemon on the side.

Scallops with celeriac and apple, cider and mustard sauce

Pan-frying scallops brings out their sweetness and is very simple and quick. Here they marry beautifully with the flavours of the celeriac, apples, cider and mustard. I've prepared the celeriac two ways – one is acidic and punchy, the other has a delicious nuttiness to it. I love the contrast in this dish, but you can opt for just one if you like.

Serves 4
10 large live scallops in the shell
1 large celeriac
Juice of 1 lemon
50ml dry cider
50ml cider vinegar
50ml water
50g sugar
Light olive oil for cooking
Cornish sea salt and freshly ground black pepper

Apple, cider and mustard sauce
2 Granny Smith apples, quartered and cored
2 tbsp English mustard
1 shallot, peeled and diced
50ml cider vinegar
100ml dry cider
2 egg yolks
Juice of ½ lemon
250ml sunflower oil

To finish
2 tbsp chopped chervil
Lemon oil (see page 214)

Shell and clean the scallops (see pages 206–7), removing the roes, then cut in half. Place in the fridge until ready to cook.

Peel and halve the celeriac. Cut one half into thick slices and immerse in cold water with the lemon juice added to avoid discoloration. Finely slice the other half, with a mandoline or very sharp knife.

Put the cider, cider vinegar, water and sugar in a pan and bring to the boil, stirring once or twice to dissolve the sugar. Add a sprinkle of salt and boil for 1 minute. Remove from the heat and add the finely sliced celeriac to this pickling liquor. Set aside to cool.

For the sauce, put the apples, all but 1 tsp of the mustard, the shallot, cider vinegar and cider in a blender and blitz for 2 minutes, then pass through a sieve into a bowl.

Put the egg yolks, lemon juice and 1 tsp mustard into a bowl and whisk to combine. Slowly whisk in the oil, drop by drop to start with, then in a steady stream, to make a thick mayonnaise. Add the puréed apple mix and stir to combine.

Drain the thick celeriac slices (of water) and pat dry. Heat a large frying pan and add a drizzle of olive oil. When hot, add the celeriac, season and cook for 3 minutes until tender and golden all over. Remove from the heat; keep warm.

Wipe out the pan, put it back on a medium heat and add a drizzle of olive oil. When hot, lay all the scallops in the pan, season with salt and pepper and cook for 1½ minutes, until golden and starting to caramelise. Remove from the heat and turn the scallops over; they will finish cooking in the residual heat of the pan.

Gently heat the sauce, whisking all the time; don't let it boil. Drain the pickled celeriac and toss with the chopped chervil.

Share the sauce equally between 4 warm plates. Arrange the pan-fried celeriac and scallops on the sauce. Finish with the pickled celeriac slices, the chopped chervil and a drizzle of lemon oil.

Scampi and ham hock with pineapple and sage

This recipe dates back to my first restaurant, The Black Pig. It may sound complicated but it is actually quite straightforward and the balance of flavours is lovely. You just need to allow time for the ham hock to cook. The dish also works very well with lobster.

Serves 4

12 large or 20 medium live scampi
Light olive oil for cooking
1 small pineapple

Ham hock

1 smoked ham hock
1 white onion, peeled and halved
2 carrots, peeled
1 garlic bulb, halved crossways
2 bay leaves
20 black peppercorns

Sage dressing

150ml white wine
150ml white wine vinegar
200ml water
75g caster sugar
100ml cold-pressed rapeseed oil
1 banana shallot, peeled and finely chopped
10 sage leaves, finely sliced
Cornish sea salt and freshly ground black pepper

To cook the ham hock, place it in a saucepan in which it fits fairly snugly with the onion, carrots, garlic, bay leaves and peppercorns and pour in enough water to cover. Slowly bring to a simmer and skim off any impurities from the surface. Cover and cook very gently for about 3 hours until the meat is very tender, topping up with water as necessary.

Bring another pan of water the boil and salt it very well. Have a bowl of iced water ready. To prepare the scampi, remove the heads and the dark intestinal tract from the tails. Blanch the scampi in the boiling water for 1 minute, then transfer to the ice-cold water. When cold, lift out and peel away the tail shells. Lay the scampi on a tray and refrigerate until ready to serve.

Peel, core and cut the pineapple into 5mm dice.

For the dressing, put the wine, wine vinegar, water and sugar in a pan and heat slowly to dissolve the sugar, then bring to the boil and boil for 1 minute. Add the diced pineapple and remove from the heat. Leave to cool.

When the pineapple has cooled, strain off the liquor and mix 8 tbsp with the rapeseed oil. Add the shallot and sage and season with a little salt.

When the ham is cooked and comes away from the bone, lift it out of the pot and leave until cool enough to handle. Strip the meat off the bone in chunky pieces; keep warm. Add 200ml of the ham liquor to the dressing.

To serve, take the scampi from the fridge and season with salt and pepper. Heat a frying pan over a medium heat and add a drizzle of oil. When hot, add the scampi tails and colour for 1 minute, turning once.

Divide the ham between 4 warm bowls, add some pineapple and spoon 4 tbsp dressing over each serving. Add the scampi tails and serve.

This may not be the healthiest of cooking methods, but there is really nothing quite like a piece of battered fresh fish deep-fried to perfection. And let's face it, you're not going to eat fish cooked this way every day, are you?

Deep-frying is, in fact, a good technique for protecting the fish and sealing in its moisture and flavour. Generally the fish is coated in batter or breadcrumbs before frying, or possibly wrapped in pastry, or – as is the custom in some countries – simply dusted with flour and dropped straight into the hot oil.

Deep-frying is considered to be a dry cooking method, because no water is used. And as the temperature of the fat or oil you use is so high, the fish or shellfish cooks quickly. What actually happens is that the high temperature of the oil heats the water within the seafood, which consequently steams – from the inside out.

You need a flavourless oil for deep-frying that doesn't interfere with the taste of the seafood – I use either sunflower or light rapeseed oil. You can reuse the oil a few times, but only for fish. Once it has cooled down, strain it before storing.

A special-purpose thermostatically controlled deep-fat fryer is convenient and easy to use, but only worth buying if you deep-fry often. A deep, heavy saucepan on the hob will suffice, but do use a cooking thermometer to check the temperature and don't fill it more than half-full.

Be careful when you are deep-frying thick pieces of fish, as a crisp golden coating may suggest they are cooked, but the heat may not have penetrated all the way through to the centre. If you think this

DEEP-FRIED

is a possibility, after frying pop the fish into a hot oven for a few minutes and it will be good to go.

When fish is deep-fried correctly, it doesn't become greasy. You'll only have this problem if the oil isn't hot enough. Obviously you need to get the oil in your deep-fryer up to the correct temperature before you add any food; the optimum temperature range for deep-frying fish is 175–190°C. Don't put too much into the pan in one go or you will bring the temperature of the oil down – cook in batches to avoid this. And don't leave the seafood in the pan once it is cooked or it will start to absorb oil.

For me, the best way to deep-fry fish is in batter. I love the contrast of a crisp, golden well-seasoned batter against the seafood. You can be creative with the batter and it can really make the most of fish varieties that are light on flavour – my crispy pollack recipe on page 174 is a good example.

I love fish and chips as long as they are crispy, and I'm not alone. Whenever I put anything deep-fried on the menu it always flies out of the kitchen!

BEST SEAFOOD TO DEEP-FRY
Pollack, cod, coley, flounder, haddock, hake, ling, whiting, lemon sole, red mullet, plaice, pouting, sprats, cuttlefish, squid, oysters, prawns, crab, queenie scallops.

ACCOMPANIMENTS & GARNISHES
Asian dipping sauce, tomato ketchup (page 215), herb mayonnaise (page 213), wasabi mayonnaise (page 134), curry mayonnaise (page 178), pickled vegetables (page 216), shoestring fries.

Fried red mullet, tarragon and garlic with tomato and anchovy dressing

Red mullet is such a beautiful fish, it's lovely to serve whole; it also tastes better cooked on the bone. Here I'm deep-frying the garnish as well as the fish. The contrasting textures work so well together and it's all finished off with a fresh, zingy tomato dressing. If you prefer to eat fish off the bone, deep-fry fillets from larger fish.

Serves 4

4 red mullet, about 400g each
4 garlic cloves, peeled and finely chopped
4 tbsp tarragon leaves, finely chopped
A little olive oil to drizzle
Oil for deep-frying
100g plain flour
Cornish sea salt and freshly ground black pepper

Tomato and anchovy dressing

3 plum tomatoes, blanched, peeled, deseeded and diced
1 tbsp white wine shallots (see page 216)
1 tbsp tarragon leaves, finely chopped
4 salted anchovy fillets, chopped
50ml lemon juice
150ml olive oil

Garnish

2 banana shallots, peeled and finely sliced
4 garlic cloves, peeled and finely sliced
Handful of tarragon leaves

Lay the red mullet in a shallow dish. Mix the garlic and tarragon together with a drizzle of olive oil and a pinch of salt. Spoon over the fish and leave to marinate for at least an hour.

Just before cooking, prepare the dressing by mixing all the ingredients together in a bowl.

Heat the oil in a deep-fat fryer or other suitable deep, heavy pan to 180°C. For the garnish, pass the sliced shallots and garlic through a third of the flour to coat and tap off any excess. In batches, fry the shallots and garlic in the hot oil for a couple of minutes until golden brown and crispy. Using a slotted spoon, transfer to a tray lined with kitchen paper and season with salt.

Next, deep-fry the tarragon leaves for about a minute until crispy, taking care as the oil will spit a little. Transfer the tarragon to the tray with the shallots and garlic. Toss together, then divide into 4 piles.

To cook the red mullet, scrape off any marinade, then dip the fish into the remaining flour to coat and tap off any excess. Carefully lower the fish into the hot oil and deep-fry for 6–7 minutes until cooked and crispy. Carefully lift out the fish and drain on kitchen paper, then season all over with salt. (If your pan isn't big enough, cook the fish in two batches, keeping the first batch warm in the oven, heated to 100°C/Gas ¼, while the second one is cooking.)

Serve the red mullet on warm plates, topped with the crispy shallots, tarragon and garlic, with the dressing in a bowl on the side.

Rosemary and cheese crumbed plaice with courgette and basil chutney

This simple dish is always popular – with children and adults alike. I've used plaice, which I love deep-fried, but you could use anything really. The chutney is just lovely to have to hand – it's great with cheese.

Serves 4

600g plaice fillet, skinned
200g stale bread, crusts removed
50g Parmesan, freshly grated
2 tsp chopped rosemary
100g plain flour to dust
2 eggs, lightly beaten
Oil for deep-frying
Cornish sea salt and freshly ground black pepper

Courgette and basil chutney

A little rapeseed oil for cooking
1 white onion, peeled and finely chopped
1 tsp mustard seeds
1 tsp onion (nigella) seeds
3 garlic cloves, peeled and chopped
1 tsp saffron strands
1 tsp chopped rosemary
150g ripe tomatoes
150ml cider vinegar
75g brown sugar
350g courgettes, diced
2 Granny Smith apples, peeled and diced
20 basil leaves, sliced

First make the chutney. Heat a large saucepan over a medium heat and add a drizzle of oil. When it is hot, add the onion, mustard and onion seeds, garlic, saffron and rosemary.

Cook for 2 minutes, then add the tomatoes, cider vinegar and brown sugar. Cook for about 20 minutes until the tomatoes collapse and the liquid becomes syrupy. Next, add the courgettes and apples and cook until the courgettes are just tender. Remove from the heat, season with salt to taste and add the basil. Leave to cool, then refrigerate unless serving straight away (the chutney will keep in a sealed jar in the fridge for up to a month).

To make the crumb coating, tear the bread into pieces and blitz in a food processor with the Parmesan, rosemary and a pinch of salt, for 1 minute. Spread the crumbs out on a tray. Get ready to crumb the fish: have the flour seasoned with salt and pepper in one bowl, the beaten eggs in another, and the tray of crumbs to hand. Heat the oil in a deep-fat fryer or other suitable deep, heavy pan to 180°C.

Deep-fry the fish, in batches if necessary: pass through the flour, then dip into the beaten eggs and finally in the breadcrumbs to coat. Add the fish to the hot oil and deep-fry for about 2 minutes until golden, then remove and drain on kitchen paper and season with a little salt.

Serve immediately, on warm plates with the chutney and some chargrilled courgettes or simply dressed salad leaves on the side.

Crispy pollack, pickled carrots and sweet vinegar dressing

As I had fallen out of love with pollack when I wrote my first book, it didn't feature but now I've let it back into my life and found some great ways to treat it. Here it is marinated with smoked paprika, coriander and lime zest before coating in batter and frying. Delicious!

Serves 4
600g pollack fillet, skinned and pin-boned
2 tbsp chopped coriander leaves
Finely grated zest of 1 lime
1 tsp smoked paprika
75g cornflour
75g plain flour, plus extra to dust
200ml ice-cold soda water
Oil for deep-frying
Cornish sea salt

Pickled carrots
3 carrots, peeled
1 banana shallot, peeled and sliced
2 garlic cloves, peeled, halved and germ removed
1 green chilli, deseeded and sliced
100ml white wine
100ml white wine vinegar
100ml water
100g caster sugar
2 spring onions, trimmed and finely sliced
1 tbsp roughly torn coriander
75ml cold-pressed rapeseed oil

To serve
Lime wedges

Cut the fish into chunks, about 4cm wide and 4cm long. Mix the chopped coriander, lime zest, smoked paprika and a good pinch of salt together in a bowl, add the fish and toss to mix. Leave to marinate for 30 minutes.

For the pickled carrots, slice the carrots into fine ribbons, using a mandoline or vegetable peeler. Place in a shallow bowl with the shallot, garlic and chilli. Heat the wine, wine vinegar, water and sugar in a pan to dissolve the sugar, then bring to a simmer and pour over the carrots. Lay a sheet of cling film over the surface to keep the carrots submerged. Leave to cool.

To make the batter, mix the cornflour and flour in a bowl with a pinch of salt. Stir in the soda water to give a smooth batter. Stand the bowl over another bowl of iced water; put to one side.

When you are ready to cook the fish, drain the pickled carrots and place them in a bowl, discarding the garlic. Add the spring onions and coriander, season with salt to taste and dress with the rapeseed oil.

Heat the oil in a deep-fat fryer or other suitable deep, heavy pan to 180°C. Toss the fish in the flour to coat and pat off any excess. Dip the pieces of fish into the batter and carefully lower them into the hot oil, one by one. Deep-fry for about 2 minutes until crisp and golden, then transfer to a tray lined with kitchen paper to drain. Season with a touch more salt.

Serve the crispy fish on a warm platter with the pickled carrot salad and lime wedges.

Crab cakes with crab custard and radish salad

A lot of people turn their nose up at brown crab meat. For me though, it's special. It's the part of the crab that has the most flavour and it's very versatile. In this dish I use it to make a custard that almost has the texture of a fine pâté. It works so well with the crab cakes, and the radishes lend a lovely crunchy contrast.

Serves 4

Crab cakes

300g fresh white crab meat, picked
   (see pages 202–3)
50g fresh brown crab meat, sieved
Light rapeseed oil for cooking
2 shallots, peeled and finely chopped
1 garlic clove, peeled and finely chopped
1 green chilli, deseeded and finely chopped
100g white breadcrumbs
1 egg, lightly beaten
2 tbsp chopped flat-leaf parsley
Oil for deep-frying
Cornish sea salt and freshly ground black pepper

Crab custard

1½ sheets of bronze leaf gelatine (4g each)
2 banana shallots, peeled and finely chopped
150g brown crab meat
30ml brandy
200ml double cream
Pinch of cayenne pepper
2 tbsp lemon juice

Radish salad

12 breakfast radishes, trimmed
3 tbsp lemon juice
6 tbsp sunflower oil
2 tsp chopped chervil leaves

To serve

Lemon wedges

To make the crab cakes, heat a frying pan over a medium heat and add a drizzle of rapeseed oil. When hot, add the shallots, garlic and chilli and cook for 2 minutes, without colouring. Remove from the pan and allow to cool.

Put the white and brown crab in a bowl with the breadcrumbs and egg. Mix well, then add the shallot mixture and parsley and season with salt and pepper to taste; mix again. Shape the mixture into small fish cakes, place on a tray and refrigerate.

For the custard, put the gelatine in a shallow bowl of cold water to soak. Heat a pan with a drizzle of oil. When it is hot, add the shallots and cook for 1 minute, then add the brown crab meat and brandy and cook for another minute. Add the cream and bring to a simmer. Transfer the mixture to a blender and add the cayenne and lemon juice. Immediately drain the gelatine leaves, squeeze out excess water and add them to the blender. Blend for 30 seconds and taste for salt, adding more if desired. Pour the crab mixture into a piping bag (or into a bowl and cover), then place in the fridge for 1 hour to set.

For the salad, chop the radishes and place in a bowl. For the dressing, whisk the lemon juice with the sunflower oil and ½ tsp salt, then use to dress the radishes. Toss through the chervil.

When ready to serve, pipe (or spoon) the crab custard into 4 small dishes. Heat the oil in a deep-fat fryer or other suitable deep, heavy pan to 180°C. Deep-fry the crab cakes, in batches if necessary: lower them into the hot oil and cook for about 2 minutes until golden. Remove and drain on a tray lined with kitchen paper.

Place a crab custard and some radish salad on each plate. Pile the crab cakes onto the plates and finish with a drizzle of the lemony dressing from the radishes. Serve with lemon wedges.

Charcoal mussels with asparagus salad and curry mayonnaise

This is a fun dish to serve as a starter or light lunch. Mussels and curry partner well, and the asparagus salad is an ideal complement.

Serves 4
2kg live mussels
100ml water
250g (2 packets) charcoal wafer biscuits
100g plain flour to dust
2 eggs, lightly beaten
Oil for deep-frying

Curry mayonnaise
2 egg yolks
1 garlic clove, peeled and chopped
30ml white wine vinegar
300ml curry oil (see page 214)

Asparagus salad
20 asparagus spears
4 tsp white wine shallots (see page 216)
2 tsp chopped coriander
1 tsp onion (nigella) seeds, toasted, plus an extra
    sprinkle to finish the mayonnaise
A little curry oil (see page 214)
Cornish sea salt

Wash the mussels and pull away the hairy beard attached to one end of the shell. Discard any that are open and refuse to close when sharply tapped, and any with damaged shells.

Place a large saucepan (one with a tight-fitting lid) over a high heat. When hot, add the mussels and pour in the water. Cover with the lid and cook for 2 minutes, or until all, or most of them, are open. Tip into a colander over a bowl to catch the liquor. When cool enough to handle,

pick out the meat from the shells; discard the shells, including any that are unopened. Let the mussel meat cool.

Finely grind the charcoal wafers in a blender. Put the flour, eggs and charcoal crumbs into separate bowls. Pass the mussels through the flour, shaking off excess, then the eggs and finally coat in the crumbs. Set aside on a tray.

For the mayonnaise, put the egg yolks, garlic and wine vinegar into a blender and blend for 30 seconds, then with the motor running, slowly add the curry oil in a steady stream. If it gets too thick, add 1 tsp water, then continue. Season with salt, spoon into a bowl and set aside.

For the salad, bring a pan of salted water to the boil. Trim the asparagus and peel the lower end of the stems, then blanch for 2 minutes. Drain and refresh in ice-cold water. Drain and pat dry. Slice the asparagus thinly on the diagonal and place in a bowl with the white wine shallots, coriander and onion seeds. Add a drizzle of curry oil, season with salt and mix gently.

Heat the oil in a deep-fat fryer or other suitable deep, heavy pan to 180°C and deep-fry the mussels, in batches as necessary, for 2 minutes until crispy. Remove and drain on kitchen paper. Sprinkle with salt.

Share the salad and mussels between plates and serve the curry mayonnaise on the side, topped with a sprinkling of onion seeds.

Cuttlefish fritters in a squid ink and red pepper sauce

Cuttlefish is an underrated fish that deserves to be used more often. I like the way that it takes on the flavours of whatever you braise it with, but doesn't lose its own character, texture or flavour.

Serves 4
600g cuttlefish, cleaned (see pages 210–11)
A little light rapeseed oil for cooking
2 white onions, peeled and finely sliced
4 garlic cloves, peeled and chopped
2 red peppers, cored, deseeded and finely diced
2 tsp smoked paprika
200ml dry cider
450ml fish stock (see page 213)
150g unsalted butter
120g plain flour, plus an extra 50g for coating
2 eggs, beaten
100g Japanese panko breadcrumbs
Oil for deep-frying
Cornish sea salt and freshly ground black pepper

Squid ink and red pepper sauce
1 large red pepper, deseeded and chopped
1 red chilli, deseeded and chopped
500ml shellfish stock (see page 213)
500ml fish stock (see page 213)
50g unsalted butter
2 ripe tomatoes, diced
4 tsp squid ink
2 tbsp chopped flat-leaf parsley

Red pepper and thyme dressing
1 red pepper
30ml cider vinegar
100ml extra virgin olive oil
2 tbsp chopped thyme

Cut the cuttlefish into 2cm slices, pat dry and season with salt and pepper.

Heat a large frying pan with a drizzle of oil, then add the cuttlefish and cook for 2 minutes, turning occasionally. Next, add the onions, garlic, red peppers and paprika and cook for 2 minutes. Pour in the cider and fish stock, bring to a simmer and cook gently for 1 hour.

For the sauce, heat a saucepan with a drizzle of oil, then add the red pepper and chilli and cook for 4 minutes. Add the stocks, butter and tomatoes, bring to the boil and reduce down to about 200ml. Transfer to a blender, add the squid ink and blitz until smooth. Pour into a bowl and stir in the parsley; set aside.

For the dressing, grill the red pepper under a high heat, or skewer on a fork and turn over a naked flame to scorch the skin, then peel. Halve, core and deseed the pepper, then cut into 1cm dice. Toss in a bowl with the cider vinegar, extra virgin oil, thyme and some salt and pepper.

When cooked, drain the cuttlefish, saving the liquor. Heat a pan over a medium heat and add the butter. When it starts to bubble, add the 120g flour, stir and cook for 2 minutes. Now add the cooking liquor, a ladleful at a time, stirring constantly to keep it smooth. Lower the heat and simmer for 20 minutes, stirring often.

Chop the cuttlefish and add to the pan. Season with salt and pepper to taste. Tip into a tray lined with greaseproof paper and let cool, then refrigerate for at least 1½ hours until set.

Cut the set cuttlefish mix into pieces, each weighing about 40g, and roll into balls. Have the beaten eggs ready in one bowl, the flour in another and breadcrumbs on a tray. Pass the cuttlefish pieces through the flour, then the eggs and finally into the breadcrumbs to coat. Set aside until ready to cook and serve.

Heat the oil in a deep-fat fryer or other suitable pan to 180°C and fry the cuttlefish, in batches as necessary, for 2–3 minutes. Meanwhile, warm the sauce. Remove the cuttlefish fritters, drain on kitchen paper and season with salt.

Serve the fritters at once, with the squid ink sauce and the red pepper and thyme dressing.

PREPARING FISH & SHELLFISH

FLAT
FISH

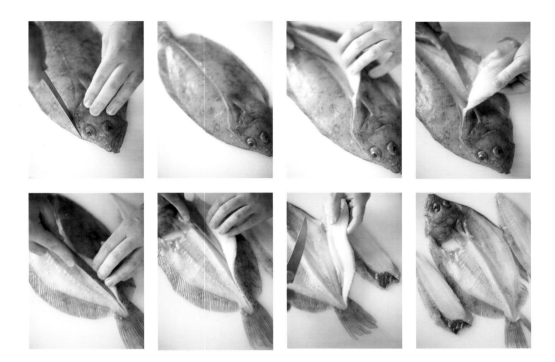

FILLETING A FLAT FISH A flat fish yields
four fillets and has two distinct sides. The top
side displays the individual characteristics of
the species – the orange spots of a plaice, or
the lumpy skin of a turbot, for example. The
underside should be a clean, creamy white.
Make sure the fish has been gutted and is as
dry as possible. Unless you've caught the fish
yourself, it will most likely be gutted. If not,
it's straightforward to do (see page 187).

Before you start filleting, make sure your
chopping board is secure by placing a damp
cloth underneath it to stop it slipping. A razor-
sharp knife is equally important; a blunt knife
will slip and is therefore dangerous.

Lay the fish on the chopping board with the
head pointing away from you. Insert your knife
at the side of the head and bring it around to
the centre of the neck. Now run the knife
down the centre bone to the end of the tail,
in one straight line. Then, starting from the
cut at the bottom of the head, carefully cut the
fillet free from the skeleton, holding the knife
flat against the bones and working towards
the edge of the fish.

When you have freed all the flesh from
the bone, cut through the skin at the tail end
and work up the edge of the fish until you reach
the top where you originally started. You should
now have released the first fillet.

To remove the second fillet, turn the fish
around so the head is pointing towards you.
Starting from the tail and working up, do
exactly the same as before until the fillet is
released. Turn the fish over and repeat on
the other side to release the other two fillets.

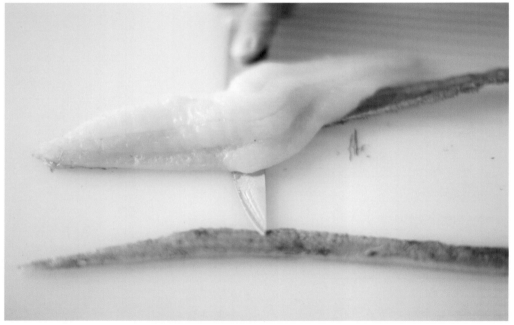

SKINNING A FLAT FISH FILLET Make sure your chopping board is secure and your knife is sharp. Lay the fillet skin side down on the board and trim away the skirt from the outer edge. (You'll find it much easier to skin the fillet if you do this first.) Now, holding the tail end down with one hand, slightly angle your knife down towards the board. Using the length of the knife and cutting smoothly, run the knife along the skin to release the fillet from it.

The aim is to leave as little flesh on the skin as possible, if any! Sometimes little bits of skin are left on the flesh, but you can just trim these away carefully.

PREPARING A FLAT FISH TO COOK WHOLE First make sure the fish has been gutted and is free from scales and sea slime. If the guts are still in place you'll find them easy to remove. They are situated just below the head and pectoral fin, so feel around with your fingers until you locate the soft innards.

Make a semi-circular cut around the edge of the gut cavity, insert your fingers into the cavity and pull the guts out. Rinse the cavity well. Now, using strong scissors, trim away the skirt from around the edge of the fish. Cut off all the fins and trim the tail.

On bigger fish like turbot you may want to remove the gills and skin, but I don't bother. I know I'm not going to eat the gills, so they do not offend me and I like to keep the skin on as it gives the fish some protection during cooking.

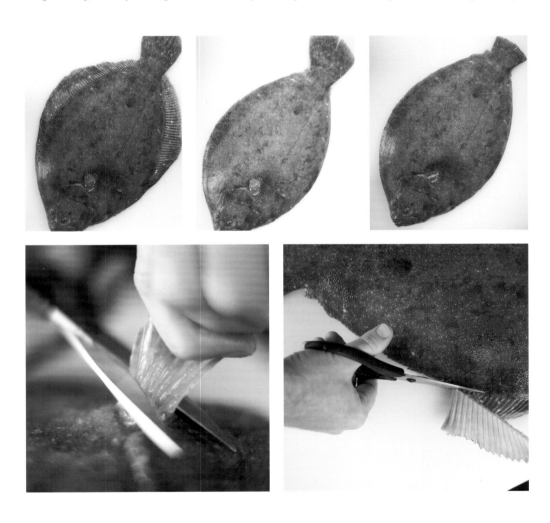

TRANCHING A FLAT FISH This is the best way to cook a big flat fish. You will need a sharp large cook's knife, kitchen scissors and a rubber mallet or old rolling pin that you don't mind getting dented.

Lay the fish on a chopping board. Remove the skirt and fins (see page 187), then cut around the head and remove it. Using the cook's knife, make a slice along the central bone from the head to the tail. The aim is to cut through this bone, so try to get the knife as central as possible. Use the mallet to give the knife a firm tap and it should go through the bone, leaving you two clean sides of fish. Next, turn the sides around and mark out the size of portion you want, slicing down to the bone at the point where you want to cut it. Obviously, you will need to adjust the intervals of your cuts, making them wider towards the tail end, to give roughly equal-sized portions.

Again hold the knife firmly against the exposed bone and hit it hard with the mallet to give you a clean quick cut. You now have a tranche ready for cooking. Repeat to cut the rest of your tranches.

Tranching is only suitable for bigger flat fish, such as turbot and brill, which yield fairly chunky portions.

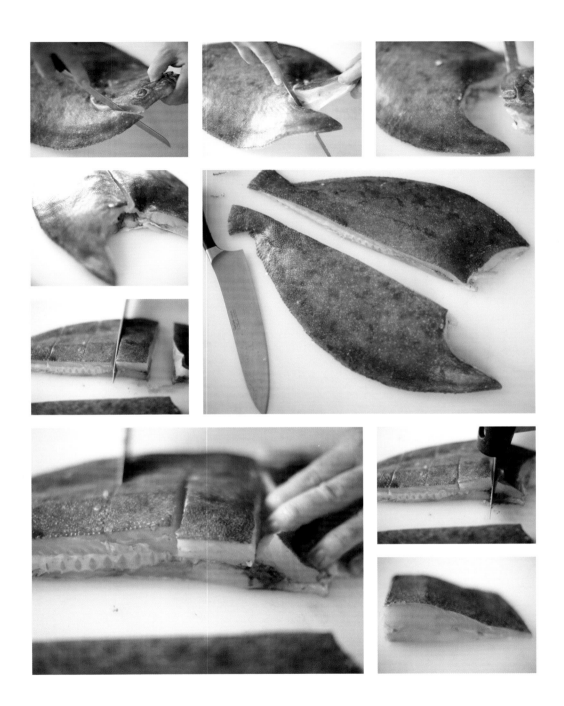

ROUND FISH

STEAKING A ROUND FISH Certain round fish really benefit from being cooked on the bone as steaks, because it seems to keep the texture firm and the fish moist – great for braising in a stew, for example.

Using a very sharp, strong knife, mark the fish at intervals where you want to portion it, then slice straight through, using a mallet to force the knife through the bone if necessary. Make sure that the portions are equal or they won't cook evenly.

DESCALING If you plan on eating your fish with the skin on – which is deliciously crisp after grilling, frying or roasting – you'll want to descale it. Most of the fish you buy will have been descaled already, or your fishmonger will offer to do it for you, but should you need to descale it yourself, it really isn't difficult. It's easiest to descale a fish when whole and to do so underwater, as this stops the scales from flying all over your kitchen.

Fill your sink with enough water to cover the fish. Now, holding the fish by the tail, submerge it in the water. Using a descaler or the back of a knife, push firmly against the skin from the tail to the head (i.e. in the opposite direction to the way the scales lie) and the scales will come off. Make sure you are careful not to push too hard as this will crush the flesh. Turn the fish over and repeat on the other side. When all the scales are off, wash and dry the fish, checking for any stray scales. It is then ready to use.

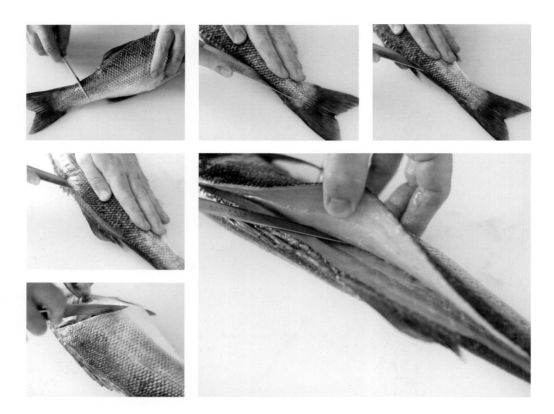

FILLETING A ROUND FISH A round fish yields two fillets. Make sure the fish has been descaled and gutted, and that all the fins and scales have been removed (see pages 191 and 195). Use a large chopping board and make sure it is firmly secure on your worktop by placing a damp cloth underneath it, and that your knife is very sharp.

Lay the fish on the board with the belly facing away from you. Make a cut at the tail end and bring the knife up along the fish, just above the backbone to the head (this cut only needs to be a few centimetres deep). When you reach the head end, cut across the fish diagonally just behind the gills, just as far as the skeleton. Now, in a firm, sweeping motion, work the knife flat across the bones from the tail to the head end, to ease the fillet away. Cut through the flesh at the tail end to release the fillet and carefully work it away from the rib cage.

To remove the second fillet you need to turn the fish over and follow the same procedure, but working from the head down to the tail. So, start by making an incision at the head end and make a shallow cut along the backbone, just above it, down to the tail.

Now carefully skim the knife over the skeleton, working smoothly from head to tail. Cut through the fillet at the head end to release the fillet and carefully work it away from the rib cage until it is free. You will now have two fillets and a clean skeleton.

PIN-BONING
Pin bones are not something that you want to get stuck in your throat, so it's always best to remove them, and is very easy to do. Lay the fish fillet on your chopping board, flesh side up. Using your fingers as a guide, feel along the centre of the fillet for any small bones. With a pair of strong tweezers, grab hold of any pin bone you find and pull firmly – towards the end where the head would have been – to remove it.

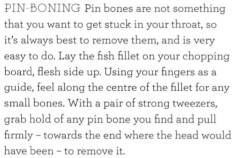

SKINNING A ROUND FISH FILLET
To skin the fillet make sure your board is secure and your knife is sharp. Lay the fillet in front of you and trim the outer edge to neaten. Now, firmly holding the skin at the tail end with one hand, slightly angle your knife down towards the board, so that when you cut into the fillet the knife will run along the skin and won't cut into the fish. Use the length of your knife as you move the knife over the skin to release the fillet from it, and avoid being aggressive with your movements. Sometimes little bits of skin get left on the fillet; just trim these off carefully.

PREPARING A ROUND FISH TO COOK WHOLE To gut the fish, if necessary, hold it belly side up in one hand with the head pointing away from you. Insert the tip of the knife at the anal vent and make a shallow cut through the flesh along the belly and up to the throat to open up the cavity. Using your hand, pull out all the guts from inside. You really do need to take care as you do this, as there may be sharp hooks and/or little spiny fish caught inside. Rinse the cavity well. Now, using strong scissors, remove all the fins and trim the tail. Cut out the gills, too. Leave the skin in place to protect the fish during cooking.

PREPARING ROUND FISH
195

BUTTERFLYING FISH This is a particularly good technique for smaller round fish, such as sardines, herring and small red mullet. If necessary, remove the guts (see page 195) and cut off the head, fins and gills. Extend the cut from gutting the fish so the fish is opened from top to tail end.

Now cut down both sides of the skeleton to release the flesh, without cutting right through. Using the palm of your hand, gently push down onto the back of the fish until the backbone is flat against the chopping board and the fillets are either side.

With most fish, you can simply pull out the backbone with your fingers, but if that isn't possible, use strong scissors and then trim off the backbone. Now use a filleting knife to trim the fish neatly and pin-bone using tweezers (see page 194). The butterflied fish is now ready to cook.

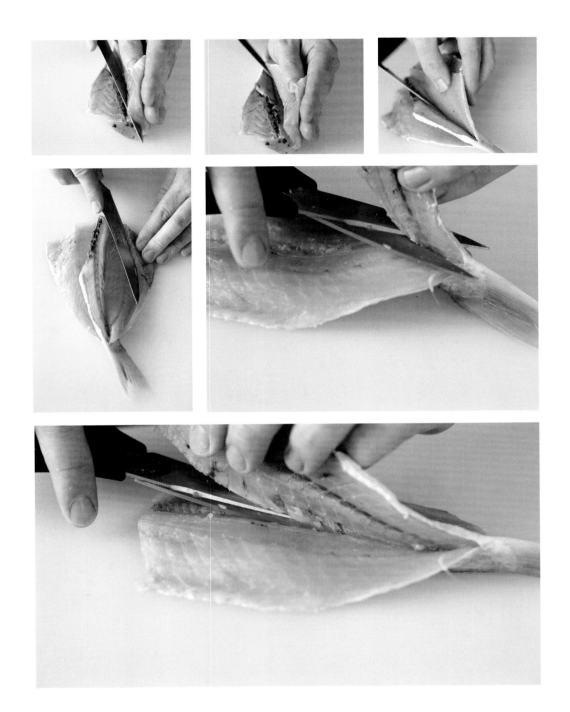

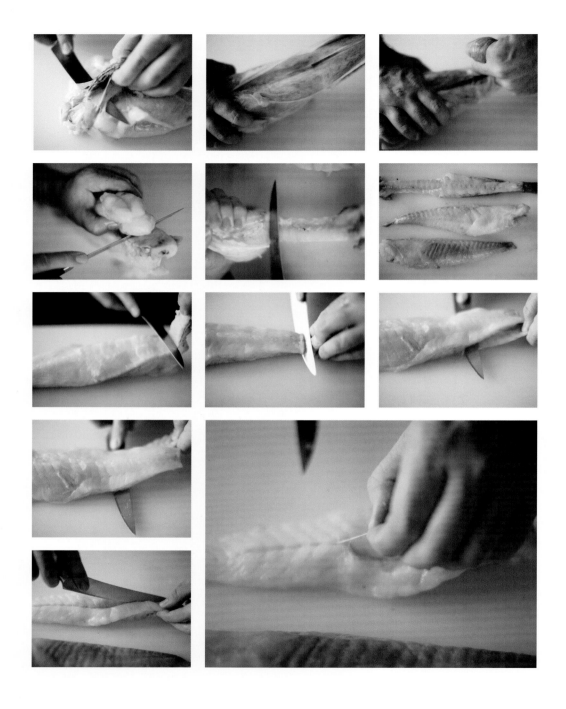

PREPARING MONKFISH Filleting monkfish is easier than other fish because it has only one central bone that runs along its entire length, but first you need to remove the skin. Take your monkfish tail and release the skin at the head end with your knife. Grasp this skin and pull towards the tail end with some force to remove the skin in one piece.

Now to fillet the monkfish, take a sharp knife and run it along one side of the bone, leaving no flesh behind on the bone. Repeat on the other side of the bone. You now have your two monkfish fillets.

Monkfish also has an inedible tough outer membrane that must be removed. As if you were skinning the fillet, grab a small bit of flesh at the tail end and cut into it. Now, holding the tail end with one hand, bring the knife from the tail to the thick end, removing as much of the membrane as possible.

Turn the fillet over and you'll expose the thin sinew in the red bloodline running along the fillet. Using the tip of your knife, cut this out. Trim off any remaining membrane. Your fish is now ready to cook.

SHELLFISH

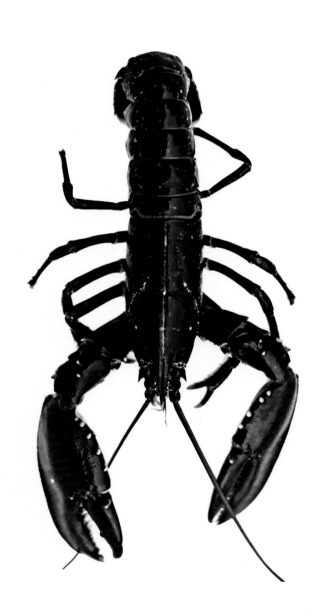

COOKING LOBSTER It is possible to kill a live lobster instantly by holding it firmly, plunging a knife into the cross on its head and splitting it lengthways quickly in two, but in reality it's quite hard to kill it with one blow. Instead I prefer to calm this crustacean first, rendering it almost comatose. The lobster may be a simple creature, with a long nerve cord rather than a brain, but it still deserves to be treated humanely.

Before boiling, I put the lobster in the freezer for about an hour until it's calmed to the point of hardly moving. Then I have a big pan of fast-boiling well-salted water ready. Use 30g salt to 1 litre water.

To cook the lobster, take it from the freezer, place it on a board and firmly insert the tip of a strong knife into the cross on the head to kill it instantly, then plunge it straight into the boiling water. Bring back to the boil. From this point, I allow 10 minutes for a lobster weighing 700g and add 1 minute for every 100g above that. For a smaller 500–600g lobster, I allow 8 minutes. When the cooking time is up, lift out the lobster and place it on a tray to cool.

PREPARING LOBSTER When the lobster is cool enough to handle, you can extract the meat. Lay it on your chopping board and split it in half lengthways from head to tail, using a large, heavy knife.

Remove the small stomach sac in the head and the dark intestinal tract that runs along the length of the tail. Don't discard the liver or 'tomalley', which is delicious. The red coral in female lobsters is good to eat too.

Tap the claws firmly with the back of a heavy knife to crack them open and release the meat. You can also pull out the meat from the thin legs.

COOKING CRAB I put crabs into the freezer an hour or so before cooking to calm them down. Also, I always try to cook my crabs in sea water, but you can use 30g salt to 1 litre tap water. If there is not enough salt in the water, flavour will leach out from the crab into the water. Bring your salty water to a fast boil.

Take the crab from the freezer and plunge an awl or other sharp pointed tool into one of the two points on its underside to kill it instantly, then plunge it into the boiling water. Once the water comes back to the boil, cook for 15 minutes if the crab is 1kg or less, adding 2 minutes for every extra 100g. As soon as the crab is cooked, lift it out onto a tray and leave until cool enough to handle.

PREPARING CRAB Remove all the legs and claws from the cooked crab, by twisting them away from the body. Now, holding the crab in both hands, use your thumbs to push the body up and out of the hard top shell.

Remove the dead man's fingers, stomach sac and hard membranes from the body shell. Using a spoon, remove the brown crab from the top shell and place in a bowl. Now cut the body in half with a sharp knife to reveal all the little channels of white crab meat. Use a crab pick or the back of a spoon to pick out all the crab meat from these crevices and put it into a bowl.

Now, with a heavy knife, break each claw with one hard tap if possible and pick out the crab meat, removing the cartilage in the middle of the claw. Do the same to extract the meat from the legs.

When you have taken out all the crab meat, go through it very carefully with your fingers a couple of times to check for any stray fragments of shell or membrane.

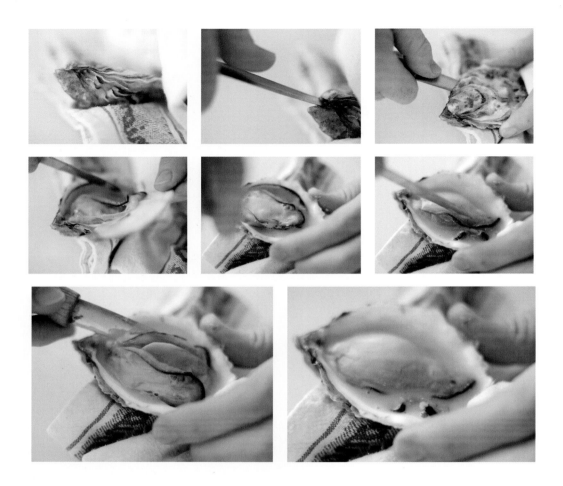

OPENING OYSTERS I find an oyster knife isn't the best implement for shucking an oyster unless you've one with a small blade; I prefer to use a sturdy butter-knife-sized knife.

Hold the oyster flat side up in a folded tea towel (for protection), in one hand. Insert the knife into the hinge of the oyster and wiggle at the hinge, using a little force, until you hear a popping sound and it yields. Run the knife along the roof of the flat side to cut the attaching muscle and release the oyster from the top shell.

Using the same knife, carefully cut away the same muscle from the bottom shell and turn the oyster over in the shell, being careful to retain all the juices. The oyster is now ready.

PREPARING RAZOR CLAMS These tasty bivalves must always be live when cooked. Rinse well, then steam them open in a covered pan with a little white wine or water. Allow to cool slightly before pulling the clams from their shells.

Now, to prepare them, cut the longer part of the clam away from the dark sac. Then cut off the rounder end, the other side of the sac. Remove the wing-like covering from the body and scrape off any sand. You can now slice both of these parts into small slices or keep them whole. Discard the dark sac.

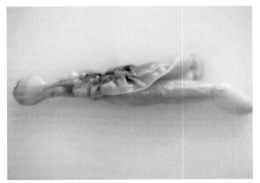

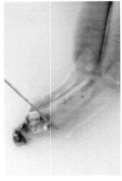
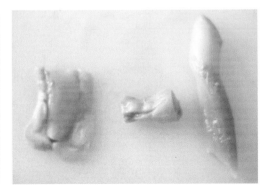

OPENING SCALLOPS This is a fun task once you get the hang of it. Make sure your scallops are alive – either tightly shut or ready to close when firmly tapped.

To open, hold the scallop firmly between the fingers and thumb of one hand, so the flatter side of the scallop shell is facing upwards. Insert the tip of a strong, fairly small knife between the shells at the corner of the hinge and twist to break it. Now bring the knife down between the shells to separate them and pull off the top shell. Using a thin, fairly flat spoon,

scrape around the scallop and the other bits until you release everything from the shell.

Now grab the scallop, roe and skirt with your hands and find the white muscle. Use your thumb and forefinger to release the scallop meat from the muscle. Work around the scallop, carefully removing the very thin membrane until you have in your hand just the white scallop meat. The plump, bright orange coral, which comes away with the muscle, can be cut free and cooked with the white scallop.

PREPARING SQUID Make sure your squid
is clean and white, with no pink tinges. Holding
the body in one hand, grab the head and pull
it firmly and carefully – the innards that are
attached to it will come away with it. If the
squid hasn't released its ink already, you'll
find the ink sac within the innards.

Pull the fins or 'wings' away from the sides
of the body. Now remove the purplish skin
covering the body. Carefully scrape the body
and fins with your knife to remove any ink
or excess skin and give the fins a quick rinse.

Returning to the head, take hold of the
tentacles and squeeze the head to remove the
sharp beak, pulling it out. Using a sharp knife,
cut the tentacles away from the head, just under
the eyes. Rinse the tentacles.

Finally, pull out the plastic-looking quill
from the body and any other insides that look
as though they shouldn't be there. Give the
body a quick rinse. At this point you can cut the
squid body open or slice it into rings. The fins
can also be cut into smaller pieces. Cook the
body, fins and tentacles as required.

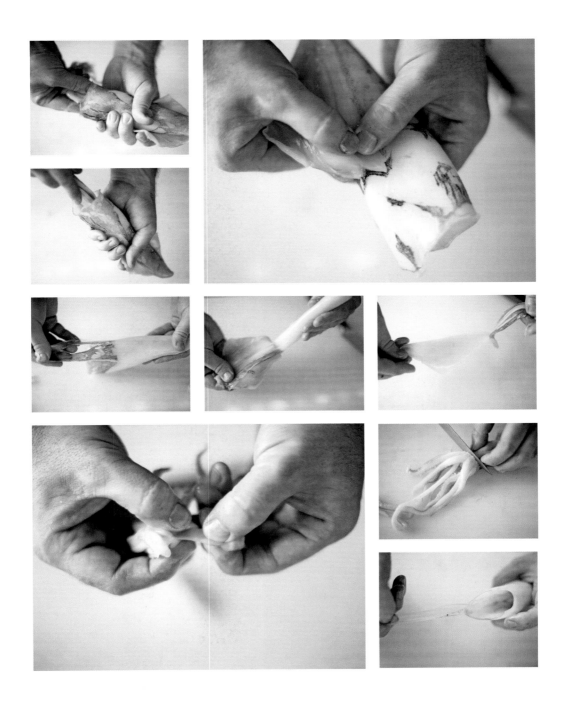

PREPARING CUTTLEFISH Using a sharp knife, cut through the hard part at the base of the head to release the cuttlebone. With your fingers, carefully push out the cuttlebone (akin to the squid's transparent quill).

Separate the head and tentacles from the body, pulling the head firmly (as you would for squid but expect more of the innards to remain inside the body). Now cautiously reach inside the body with your hand to release the innards, taking great care to avoid rupturing the ink sac if it is still intact, otherwise you will end up in a dreadful mess!

Returning to the head, squeeze out the beak and cut off the tentacles at the eyes. Finally peel away the skin from the body – you will find this quite easy to do.

Cuttlefish can be cooked in the same way as squid, though I much prefer to braise them slowly to tenderise their thicker, tougher flesh.

BASIC
RECIPES

FISH STOCK

<u>Makes about 500ml</u>
1kg turbot, brill or sole bones, washed and
   all blood removed

Preheat your oven to 200°C/Gas 6. Line a roasting tray with silicone paper and lay the fish bones on it. Roast for 30 minutes, then turn the bones over and roast for another 10 minutes.

Transfer the roasted bones to a stockpot and pour on enough water to cover. Bring to a simmer over a medium heat and skim off any impurities from the surface. Simmer for 30 minutes, then take off the heat and strain through a sieve into another pan. Bring the stock back to a simmer and reduce by half. Remove from the heat and allow to cool. The stock is now ready to use. You can store it in the fridge for up to 3 days or freeze it for up to 2 months.

SHELLFISH STOCK

<u>Makes about 500ml</u>
1kg frozen shell-on prawns
Olive oil for cooking
2 onions, peeled and chopped
3 carrots, peeled and chopped
6 ripe tomatoes, chopped
6 garlic cloves, peeled and chopped
Finely pared zest and juice of 1 orange

Preheat your oven to 200°C/Gas 6. Put the frozen prawns on a roasting tray and roast for 30 minutes. Meanwhile, heat a large pan over a medium heat, add a little olive oil and sweat the onions, carrots, tomatoes, garlic and orange zest for 5 minutes until lightly coloured. Once the prawns are roasted, chop them and add to the pan. Pour on enough water to cover and add the orange juice. Bring to a simmer and simmer for 1 hour. Strain through a sieve into another pan. Simmer to reduce by half. Remove from the heat and allow to cool. The stock is now ready to use. You can store it in the fridge for up to 2 days or freeze it for up to a month.

Crab stock: Replace the prawns with 1kg live shore crabs. Prepare for cooking as for crab (see page 202). Roast for an extra 15 minutes.

Lobster stock: Replace the prawns with 1kg lobster shells and heads.

MAYONNAISE

<u>Makes about 350ml</u>
3 egg yolks
1 tsp English mustard
Juice of ½ lemon or 2 tsp white wine vinegar or
   cider vinegar
300ml light rapeseed oil
Cornish sea salt and freshly ground
   black pepper

Put the egg yolks, mustard and lemon juice or wine (or cider) vinegar into a bowl and whisk together for 1 minute. Now slowly add the oil, drop by drop to begin with, then in a steady stream, whisking constantly, until the mixture is emulsified and thick.

Alternatively, you can make the mayonnaise in a blender or food processor, blending the egg yolks, mustard and lemon juice or vinegar for 1 minute and then adding the oil slowly through the funnel with the motor running.

Season the mayonnaise with salt and pepper to taste. Cover and refrigerate until needed. It will keep in the fridge for a couple of days.

Herb mayonnaise: Add 3–4 tbsp chopped herbs of your choice to the finished mayonnaise. Dill, tarragon and parsley are good options with fish.

Mustard mayonnaise: For an extra mustardy kick, use 2 tsp English mustard rather than 1 tsp.

LEMON OIL

Makes about 400ml
Finely pared zest of 4 unwaxed lemons
300ml light rapeseed oil
100ml light olive oil

Put all of the ingredients into a blender and blitz for 2 minutes. Pour the oil mixture into a jug and leave to infuse and settle for 24 hours. Decant the oil into another container. Keep in the fridge and use within a month.

Orange oil: Use the zest of 4 oranges rather than lemons.

BASIL OIL

Makes about 150ml
30g basil leaves
30g flat-leaf parsley leaves
150ml light olive oil
Cornish sea salt

Bring a pan of salted water to a simmer and get a bowl of iced water ready. When the water is simmering, add the herbs and blanch for 30 seconds. Immediately scoop out the herbs and plunge them straight into the iced water to cool quickly. Drain and squeeze out all excess water.

Put the blanched herbs into a blender with the olive oil and blitz for 2 minutes. Transfer the mixture to a container, cover and refrigerate for at least 3–4 hours, preferably overnight.

Warm the oil slightly and then pass it through a sieve into a clean container. The oil is now ready to use. It will keep in the fridge for a week.

Dill oil: Replace the basil and parsley with 60g dill leaves.

WILD GARLIC OIL

Makes about 200ml
60g wild garlic leaves
40g spinach
200ml light rapeseed oil
Cornish sea salt

Bring a pan of salted water to a simmer and get a bowl of iced water ready. When the water is simmering, add the wild garlic leaves and spinach and blanch for 30 seconds. Immediately scoop out the leaves and plunge them straight into the iced water to cool quickly. Drain and squeeze out all excess water.

Put the blanched leaves in a blender with the rapeseed oil and blitz for 2 minutes. Transfer to a container, cover and refrigerate for at least 3–4 hours, preferably overnight.

Warm the oil slightly and pass through a sieve into a clean container. It is now ready to use and will keep in the fridge for a week.

CURRY OIL

Makes about 400ml
4 tsp mild curry powder
400ml light rapeseed oil

Sprinkle the curry powder into a dry frying pan and toast over a medium heat for 1–2 minutes until it releases its aroma; don't let it burn. Pour the oil into the pan and remove from the heat. Give it a good stir and then pour it into a jug. Leave to infuse and settle for 24 hours, then decant the curry oil into another container. It will keep for 3 months in a dark cupboard.

TOMATO KETCHUP

Olive oil for cooking
2 red onions, peeled and chopped
6 garlic cloves, peeled and sliced
20 black peppercorns
2.5kg ripe tomatoes, roughly chopped
100g caster sugar
4 tsp chopped thyme
1 cinnamon stick
4 bay leaves
300ml red wine vinegar
Cornish sea salt and freshly ground
    black pepper

Heat a large saucepan over a medium heat and add a drizzle of olive oil. When hot, add the onions and garlic and cook for 2 minutes until the onions start to turn translucent.

Meanwhile, tie the peppercorns in a piece of muslin. Add the tomatoes, sugar, thyme, cinnamon, bay leaves and peppercorn bundle to the pan and cook for 15 minutes until the tomatoes have broken down. Continue to cook until the tomato liquid has reduced right down, almost to nothing.

Now add the wine vinegar and let bubble for 5 minutes. Remove the cinnamon, bay leaves and peppercorn bundle.

Tip the contents of the pan into a blender or food processor and blend until smooth, then pass though a sieve into a bowl. Taste for seasoning, adding salt and pepper as required.

Transfer the ketchup to a clean container and allow to cool, then seal. It will keep in the fridge for up to a week; alternatively you can freeze it for up to a month.

MUSHROOM KETCHUP

Makes 200ml (enough for 6 servings)
Olive oil for cooking
1 white onion, peeled and chopped
4 garlic cloves, peeled and finely chopped
2 bay leaves
500g button mushrooms, finely sliced
100ml white wine
100ml white wine vinegar
500ml vegetable stock
50g soft brown sugar
Cornish sea salt and freshly ground
    black pepper

Heat a large saucepan over a medium heat and add a drizzle of olive oil. When hot, add the onion, garlic and bay leaves and sweat for 2 minutes. Add the mushrooms and cook until they are starting to colour and all the juices they release have evaporated and the pan is quite dry.

Add the wine and let bubble until reduced by half, then add the wine vinegar and again reduce by half. Finally add the stock and sugar, stir to dissolve and simmer until the liquid has reduced right down, almost to nothing.

Transfer the mixture to a blender and blend until smooth. Taste for seasoning, adding salt and pepper as required.

Transfer the ketchup to a clean container and allow to cool, then seal. It will keep in the fridge for up to a week; alternatively you can freeze it for up to a month.

PICKLED ONIONS

Serves 6
2 medium onions
100ml dry white wine
100ml white wine vinegar
100ml water
100g caster sugar
2 bay leaves
10 black peppercorns

Peel the onions, cut into wedges, then separate the layers into petals. Put all the ingredients, except the onions, into a saucepan and bring to a simmer over a medium heat. Add the onions, take off the heat and allow to cool. Transfer to a kilner jar or airtight container, seal and leave for at least 24 hours, preferably a week before using.

Kept in a sterilised jar in the fridge, these pickled onions will be good for 3 months.

RED WINE SHALLOTS

Serves 10
4 large banana shallots, peeled
150ml red wine
75ml red wine vinegar
75g caster sugar
Cornish sea salt

Slice the shallots into fine rings and place in a clean container. Put the wine, wine vinegar and sugar into a saucepan and bring to a simmer over a medium heat.

Add a pinch of salt. Pour the hot pickling liquor over the shallots, make sure they are submerged and leave to cool. Seal and leave for at least 12 hours before using.

Stored in a sterilised jar in the fridge, these pickled shallots will keep for 3 months.

White wine shallots: Finely chop rather than slice the shallots. Proceed as above, using white instead of red wine and wine vinegar.

PICKLED VEGETABLES

Serves 4
1 fennel bulb, tough outer layer removed
2 banana shallots, peeled and finely sliced
2 carrots, peeled and finely sliced
2 celery sticks, de-stringed and sliced
1 thyme sprig
1 garlic clove, peeled and crushed
100ml white wine
100ml white wine vinegar
100ml water
100g caster sugar
Cornish sea salt and freshly ground
    black pepper

Cut the fennel into wafer-thin slices, ideally using a mandoline. Put into a large bowl with the rest of the vegetables, thyme and garlic. Bring the wine, wine vinegar, water and sugar to a simmer over a medium heat, stirring.

Simmer for 1 minute, then pour this pickling liquor over the vegetables. Season with salt and pepper. Transfer to a clean container, seal and leave for at least 12 hours before serving.

Stored in a sterilised jar in the fridge, these pickled vegetables will keep for a month.

Spiced pickled vegetables: Replace the fennel and thyme with 1 thinly sliced red pepper, ½ red chilli, deseeded, and 1 tsp fennel seeds. Discard the chilli before serving.

OVEN-DRIED TOMATOES

Serves 6
8 ripe plum tomatoes
2 garlic cloves, peeled and sliced
2 thyme sprigs, picked and chopped
100ml olive oil
Caster sugar, to taste
Cornish sea salt and freshly ground
    black pepper

Heat your oven to 110°C/Gas ¼. Bring a large pan of salted water to a simmer on a medium heat. Immerse the tomatoes in the water for 20 seconds and then remove with a slotted spoon and plunge straight into a bowl of iced water to cool quickly. Take out the tomatoes and peel away the skins.

Quarter the tomatoes lengthways. Using a small knife, cut out the core and seeds and lay the tomatoes cut side up on a foil-lined tray. Sprinkle over the garlic, thyme and olive oil, then season with salt, pepper and sugar. Place in the oven for 1 hour, then turn the tomatoes over and cook for a further 45 minutes.

If not using straight away, layer the tomatoes in a tub or jar and cover with olive oil. They will keep in the fridge for up to a week.

CRISPY FRIED CAPERS

Makes 4 tsp
4 tsp large capers in brine, drained
Oil for deep-frying
Cornish sea salt

Pat the capers dry with kitchen paper. Heat a 3cm depth of oil in a suitable deep, heavy pan to 180°C. Drop the capers into the hot oil and deep-fry for 1 minute until crispy. Drain on kitchen paper and sprinkle with a little salt.

CRISPY FRIED SHALLOTS

Serves 4
2 large banana shallots, peeled and thinly sliced
Oil for deep-frying
Cornish sea salt

To cook the shallots, heat the oil in a deep-fryer or other suitable deep, heavy pan to 180°C and your oven to 120°C/Gas ½. Deep-fry the shallots in the hot oil until golden.

Transfer the shallots to an oven tray and place in the oven for 30 minutes to dry out and crisp up. Drain on kitchen paper and season with a little salt. Serve hot.

CRISPY FRIED SEAWEED

Serves 4
4 large handfuls of seaweed (ideally gutweed),
    well washed, or finely sliced greens or
    Savoy cabbage
Oil for deep-frying
Cornish sea salt

To cook the seaweed, heat the oil in a deep-fryer or other suitable deep, heavy pan to 200°C. Dry the seaweed (or greens) thoroughly by squeezing in a tea towel or cloth to remove all water. Deep-fry in the hot oil in small batches for 2 minutes until crispy. Drain on kitchen paper and season with a little salt. Serve hot.

WHITE BREAD

Makes 1 loaf or 5–10 rolls (depending on size)
250g white bread flour
60g fermented starter dough (see right)
150ml water
15g fresh yeast
15g unsalted butter
10g fine sea salt

Put all the ingredients, except the salt, into an electric mixer fitted with a dough hook and mix on a high speed for 6 minutes. Add the salt and mix for another 2 minutes. Transfer the dough to a floured bowl, cover with a damp cloth and leave to rise in a warm place for 30 minutes. On a floured surface, knock back the risen dough. The dough is now ready to shape, either into loaves or rolls.

To shape and bake a loaf: Shape into a round or other loaf shape and place on a baking sheet, or form into an oblong and place in a standard 500g loaf tin. Cover with a damp cloth and leave to prove in a warm place until doubled in size, about 40 minutes. Meanwhile, heat the oven to 220°C/Gas 7.

Sprinkle the surface of the loaf with flour. Bake for 20 minutes or until golden brown and the loaf sounds hollow when tapped on the underside. Transfer to a wire rack and leave to cool before serving.

To shape and bake rolls or burger buns: Divide the bread dough into 50g balls (or 100g balls for burger buns). The best way to do this is to use electric scales. On a floured surface, take a portion of dough and using both hands and fingertips, bring the dough from the bottom to the top and turn the dough over. Now, using the sides of both hands, roll the dough in a circle until you have a smooth round roll. Repeat to shape the rest. Place on a floured baking tray, cover with a damp cloth and leave to prove in a warm place until doubled in size, about 40 minutes. Meanwhile, heat the oven to 220°C/Gas 7.

Sprinkle the rolls with flour and bake for 12–15 minutes or until golden brown. Cool on a wire rack before serving.

Fermented starter dough: I use this 'starter dough' for most of my breads. It lends an incredible depth of flavour. A couple of days in advance, open a 400g tin of peaches or pears, tip into a bowl, cover and leave to ferment for 2 days. Once fermented, transfer the fruit and juice to a blender and blitz to a smooth liquid, then pass through a sieve into a jug. Put 280g white bread flour, 15g fresh yeast and 160ml of the fermented juice into an electric mixer fitted with a dough hook and mix on a high speed until a smooth dough has formed. Transfer to a lidded container. The fermented 'starter' dough will live in the fridge happily for up to 5 days... but keep an eye on it as it might try to escape! (Makes enough for 4 loaves)

TREACLE BREAD

Makes 2 loaves
250g white bread flour
250g granary bread flour
200ml water
30g fresh yeast
30g unsalted butter
100g black treacle
15g fine sea salt

Put all the ingredients, except the salt, into an electric mixer fitted with a dough hook and mix on a high speed for 6 minutes. Add the salt and mix for another 2 minutes. Transfer the dough to a floured bowl, cover with a damp cloth and leave to rise in a warm place for 30 minutes.

On a floured surface, knock back the risen dough. Divide in half and shape each piece into a loaf. Cover with a damp cloth and leave to prove in a warm place until doubled in size, about 40 minutes. Meanwhile, heat the oven to 220°C/Gas 7.

Sprinkle the surface of the loaves with flour. Bake for 20 minutes or until golden brown and the loaf sounds hollow when tapped on the underside. Transfer to a wire rack and leave to cool before serving.

SQUID INK BREAD

Makes 2 loaves
250g white bread flour
60g fermented starter dough (see left)
100ml water
15g fresh yeast
15g unsalted butter
10g fine sea salt
100ml squid ink

Put all the ingredients, except the salt and squid ink, into an electric mixer fitted with a dough hook and mix on a high speed for 6 minutes. Add the salt and squid ink and mix for another 2 minutes.

Transfer the dough to a floured bowl, cover with a damp cloth and leave to rise in a warm place for 30 minutes.

On a floured surface, knock back the risen dough. Divide in half and shape each piece into a loaf. Cover with a damp cloth and leave to prove in a warm place until doubled in size, about 40 minutes. Meanwhile, heat the oven to 220°C/Gas 7.

Sprinkle the surface of the loaves with flour. Bake for 20 minutes or until golden brown and the bread sounds hollow when tapped on the underside. Transfer to a wire rack and leave to cool before serving. This bread freezes well.

SEAWEED AND STOUT BREAD

Makes 2 loaves
250g white bread flour
250g granary bread flour
30g fresh yeast
30g unsalted butter
2 tbsp dried sea lettuce
2 tbsp dried dulse
200ml Guinness
100ml water
15g fine sea salt

Put all the ingredients, except the salt, into an electric mixer fitted with a dough hook and mix on a high speed for 6 minutes. Add the salt and mix for another 2 minutes. Transfer the dough to a floured bowl, cover with a damp cloth and leave to rise in a warm place for 30 minutes.

On a floured surface, knock back the risen dough. Divide in half and shape each piece into a loaf. Cover with a damp cloth and leave to prove in a warm place until doubled in size, about 40 minutes. Meanwhile, heat the oven to 220°C/Gas 7.

Sprinkle the surface of the loaves with flour and place on a lightly greased baking tray. Bake for 20 minutes or until golden brown and the loaf sounds hollow when tapped on the underside. Transfer to a wire rack and leave to cool before serving. This bread freezes well.

Note: The dried seaweeds can be obtained by mail order from online suppliers.

INDEX

ACKNOWLEDGEMENTS

There are so many people that help me every day and I certainly wouldn't have been able to write a book like this or run my restaurants without them. Those mentioned below are the ones who have supported me the most in writing this book and I owe a big hug and thanks to you all...

My wife Rachel, son Jacob and daughter Jessica, you guys are the best. Your love and support keep me going and make me try to get better at what I do, so we can all have a great life together. And Bud the Lurcher, always there and happy to see me whatever the time!

Mum, thank you for all the support and for keeping me going to the right place at the right time, most of the time! Your help with this book is hugely appreciated, thank you.

Dad, thanks for being dad!

Chris Simpson, my head chef and friend, for staying sharp in the kitchen of Restaurant Nathan Outlaw. Your input for this book will never be forgotten. Thank you.

Tim Barnes, thanks for all your help with the book and for truly amazing stories and special comments (you ain't never right!) to add to this book. And to Georgie Dent for always staying strong.

The RNO front of house team: Stephi and Damon Little, Charlie Little, Julia Krause, Carmen Kostenzer and also Deano Medlan. Thank you forever.

At Outlaw's, Rock: Redas Katauskas, Tom 'Barnes' Brown, Daniel Southern, Anna Davey and Jorge Monteiro. Thank you for keeping Outlaw's sailing through the Cornish seas. And to Christian Sharp, Andrew Snell, Shane Hodges, Emma Meech and Rosie Kimbrell – amazing!

At Outlaw's Fish Kitchen, a big thank you to Paul Ripley and to James Lean, Megan Rees, Faye Nicholson.

At Outlaw's at The Capital and The Capital Hotel, thank you to everyone, in particular my generals: Pete Biggs and Sharon McArthur. You are great!

Also to Karen de Salis and Sarah Partridge (on computers, phones and tea!), David Hunter, Kim and Tina Oxenham and Kate Simms, for your terrific behind-the-scenes work.

To Ian Dodgson, my general manager, massive thanks for all your support... there aren't many people who can eat more cake than me!

At Quadrille I would like to thank Anne Furniss, for once again believing in me and letting me write another book about the subject I love, and the amazing Helen Lewis for creating such a lovely, fresh and vibrant looking book.

Also the most patient editor on the planet, Janet Illsley, I firstly thank you for everything and secondly apologise for missing every deadline you set. Naughty boy! I'm very grateful to designer Arielle Gamble for making it all look so good on the page too.

David Loftus, what can I say! The photos once again look fantastic and it was such a pleasure to work with you on my second book.

And to Heston Blumenthal for writing the foreword. Thank you very much indeed!

Finally, to all the people who bought *Nathan Outlaw's British Seafood*, tried the recipes and sent me your photos and comments, inspiring me to write a second book. Thank you so much and I hope you like *Nathan Outlaw's Fish Kitchen* too!

Editorial director Anne Furniss
Creative director Helen Lewis
Project editor Janet Illsley
Design and illustrations Arielle Gamble
Photographer David Loftus
Food for photography Nathan Outlaw
Production Sasha Hawkes, Vincent Smith

This edition first published in 2018 by Quadrille, an imprint of Hardie Grant Publishing

Quadrille
52–54 Southwark Street
London
SE1 1UN
quadrille.com

Text © 2014 Nathan Outlaw
Photography © 2014 David Loftus
Design and layout © 2014 Quadrille Publishing Limited

Cataloguing in Publication Data: a catalogue record for this book is available from the British Library.

ISBN 978 1 78713 266 5

Printed in China